600 Jahre Universität Leipzig
600 Years of Leipzig University

LEIPZIGER VOLKSZEITUNG

IMPRESSUM IMPRINT

600 Jahre Universität Leipzig – Aus Tradition Grenzen überschreiten
600 Years of Leipzig University – A Tradition of Crossing Boundaries
1. Auflage, Juni 2009, ISBN 978-3-9811948-5-2
1st edition, June 2009, ISBN 978-3-9811948-5-2

Verlag **Publisher:** Leipziger Medien Service GmbH
Herausgeber **Editor:** Universität Leipzig
Projektleitung **Project management:** Thomas Seidler, Tobias D. Höhn
Schlussredaktion **Copy editor:** Dr. Jens Blecher
Texte **Text:** Jörg Aberger, Tobias D. Höhn, Thomas Seidler
Übersetzung **Translation:** Ines Laue, Joni Smith
Titelfoto **Cover photo:** Jan Woitas
Wachsabdruck des Großen Siegels der Universität Leipzig von 1409
Wax cast of the Great Seal of the University of Leipzig from 1409
Fotos **Photos:** Archiv, Kustodie und Pressestelle der Universität Leipzig, Leipziger Volkszeitung, Stadtgeschichtliches Museum, Deutsche Presse-Agentur
Buchgestaltung **Book design:** GrafikDesign Sabine Frohmader
Druck **Printed by:** Druckhaus Göttingen

Die Deutsche Nationalbibliothek verzeichnet diese Publikation in der Deutschen Nationalbibliografie; detaillierte bibliografische Daten sind im Internet über http://dnb.ddb.de abrufbar.
This publication is listed in the *Deutsche Nationalbibliografie* at the German National Library; detailed bibliographical references are available on the Internet at http://dnb.ddb.de

600 Jahre Universität Leipzig
600 Years of Leipzig University

Aus Tradition Grenzen überschreiten A Tradition of Crossing Boundaries

1409 2009 . 1409 2009 . 1409 2009 . 1409 2009 . 1409 2009 . 1409 2009 . 1409 2009 . 1409 2009 . 1409 2009 . 1409 2009 . 1409 2009 . 1409 2009 . 1409 2009 . 1409 2009

INHALT CONTENTS

VORWORT FOREWORD

Liebe Leserinnen, liebe Leser, als ehemaliger Student und nun Ehrendoktor der Juristenfakultät der Alma mater Lipsiensis erfüllt es mich mit großer Freude, »meiner« Universität zum 600. Gründungstag gratulieren zu können. Keine andere deutsche Hochschule hatte eine ebenso wechselvolle wie bewegende Geschichte zu überstehen wie die Universität Leipzig. Sie überlebte Kriege, politische Wirren und Regime, sie entwickelte sich über Jahrhunderte zu einer der renommiertesten Lehr- und Forschungseinrichtungen.

1409 waren es wenige Magister und Scholaren, die von Prag nach Leipzig auszogen, um hier einen akademischen Neuanfang zu wagen. Von Beginn an war die Universität im Herzen der Stadt zuhause, durch den futuristischen Campus-Neubau am Augustusplatz wird dieses Bekenntnis bekräftigt. Der Gebäudekomplex erinnert an die Vergangenheit und weist den Weg in die Zukunft, getreu dem Leitmotto der Universität »Aus Tradition Grenzen überschreiten«.

Dieses Buch möchte Ihnen einen kleinen Einblick in die Geschichte der zweitältesten Universität in Deutschland geben, erzählt vom Studenten- und Professorenalltag früherer Zeiten. Es porträtiert den Aufstieg einer Institution, die Johann Wolfgang von Goethe, Gottfried Wilhelm Leibniz, die Nobelpreisträger Werner Heisenberg und Wilhelm Ostwald magisch anzog. Die Liste prominenter Studenten und Gelehrter ist lang. Die Hauptrolle spielen jedoch die Studenten. Fast 30 000 junge Menschen aus 150 Staaten sind gegenwärtig immatrikuliert. Sie machen die Universität Leipzig zu einer festen Größe im Netzwerk internationaler Bildungseinrichtungen. Dass die Universität Leipzig weltweit bekannt ist, wurde mir auch auf vielen Reisen als Bundesaußenminister immer wieder bewusst. Ich bin sicher, ihre Erfolgsgeschichte wird fortgeschrieben.

Dear Reader, as a former student and now honorary doctor of the Faculty of Law at the Alma mater Lipsiensis, I take great pleasure in congratulating "my" University on the 600th anniversary of its foundation. No other German institution of higher education had to endure such a changing and moving history as the University of Leipzig. It survived wars, political disturbances and regimes and it developed into one of the most renowned institutions of teaching and research over the centuries.

In 1409, there were a few students and masters who left Prague to attempt a new academic beginning here in Leipzig. Right from the start, the University had its home in the heart of the city, a commitment which is confirmed by the futuristic new campus in the *Augustusplatz* square. This complex of buildings commemorates the past and points the way to the future, faithful to the University's guiding principle "A Tradition of Crossing Boundaries".

This book wishes to deliver insight into the history of the second oldest University in Germany. It gives an account of the daily lives of students and professors in earlier times. It portrays the rise of an institution which had a magical attraction to Johann Wolfgang von Goethe, Gottfried Wilhelm Leibniz and the Nobel Prize Laureates Werner Heisenberg and Wilhelm Ostwald. The list of illustrious students and scholars is long. The main role, however, is played by the students. Almost 30,000 young people from 150 countries are currently enrolled. They make the University of Leipzig an established constant within the network of international educational institutions. I was repeatedly reminded of the world renown of Leipzig University on my many journeys as Federal Foreign Minister. I am sure that its success story will continue.

Hans-Dietrich Genscher
Bundesminister a. D.

AUSZUG, KARGE KOST UND KRAWALLE VORM HAUS DES REKTORS

DEPARTURE, SCANT MEALS AND RIOTS IN FRONT OF THE RECTOR'S HOUSE

Sie hat nur rund 300 Worte, die Verfügung, die der böhmische König Wenzel IV. am 18. Januar 1409 erlässt, doch sie ist von ungeheurer Sprengkraft: Mit dem Kuttenberger Dekret kehrt er die bis dahin geltenden Stimmenverhältnisse in den Gremien der Prager Karls-Universität glatt um. Seit Gründung der Universität verfügen die so genannten Nationen der Böhmen, Bayern, Sachsen und Polen, die man auch als Landsmannschaften bezeichnen kann, jeweils über eine Stimme. Nun ordnet Wenzel an, dass die Böhmen drei Stimmen erhalten, während die anderen Nationes nur insgesamt eine Stimme bekommen.

Doch damit nicht genug: Am 9. Mai werden dem Rektor der Universität, Magister Henning Boltenhagen, und dem Dekan der Philosophischen Fakultät, Magister Albert Bärentrapp, die Studentenverzeichnisse sowie Siegel und Schlüssel der Prager Universität abgenommen. Die nichtböhmischen Studenten und Hochschullehrer reagieren auf diesen Eklat mit dem Auszug aus Prag. Allerdings darf man sich dies bestimmt nicht so vorstellen, wie es eine Postkarte aus dem Jahr 1909 illustriert: eine Heerschar von Studenten und Magistern, die sich gemeinsam auf den Weg nach Leipzig machen. Ein solcher Tross von Menschen hätte unterwegs vermutlich kaum Aufnahme in Klöstern gefunden, auf deren Gastfreundschaft die Wanderer aber angewiesen sind. Wahrscheinlicher ist, dass sich die Lehrer und ihre Schüler in kleineren Grüppchen nach Leipzig begeben.

The decree ordered by the Bohemian King Wenceslas IV on 18 January 1409 numbered no more than 300 words, but its explosive force was enormous. The Decree of Kutná Hora clearly shook up the distribution of votes applying to the institutional bodies within Charles University in Prague. Since the foundation of the University, the so-called Bohemian, Bavarian, Saxon and Polish *nationes,* which can also be referred to as regional student corporations, held one vote each. At this point, Wenzeslas ordered the Bohemians be granted three votes, while the other *nationes* collectively be given only one.

As if that were not enough, on 9 May, the student registries, as well as the seal and the key to Prague University were taken from both the Rector, Magister Henning Boltenhagen, and the Dean of the Faculty of Philosophy, Magister Albert Bärentrapp. The foreign students and professors reacted to this scandal by emigrating from Prague. And this withdrawal would have looked nothing like the way in which it was depicted in a 1909 postcard that shows a host of students and masters embarking on their way to Leipzig together. The wanderers depended on the hospitality of monasteries, however, such a large group of people would not likely have found shelter there. It is more conceivable that the instructors and their students headed for Leipzig in smaller groups.

Universitätssiegel mit Heiligem Laurentius und Johannes dem Täufer auf Konsolen unter gotischem Baldachin.
University Seal with Saint Lawrence and John the Baptist on corbels beneath a gothic canopy.

Madonna mit Kind auf dem »Kleinen Universitätssiegel« des Rektors.
Madonna with child on the "Small University Seal" of the Rector.

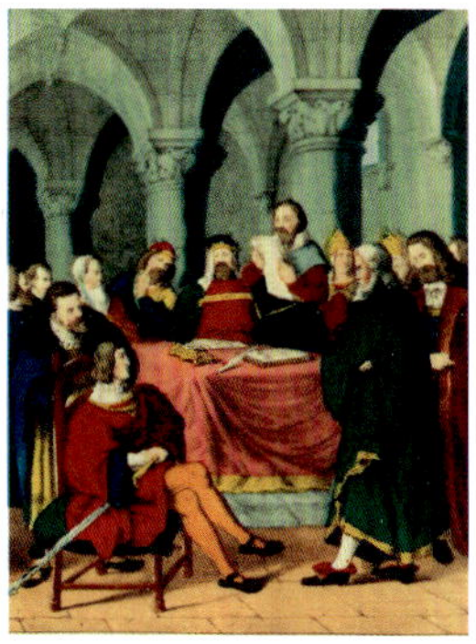

Gründung der Universität am 2. Dezember 1409 im Thomaskloster.
Foundation of the University on 2 December 1409 in St. Thomas Monastery.

GENEHMIGUNG VOM PAPST

Bis es zur tatsächlichen Gründung der Leipziger Universität kommt, vergeht erstaunlich wenig Zeit. Schon im September 1409 erteilt Papst Alexander V. die Genehmigung zur Errichtung der Alma mater Lipsiensis, und Markgraf Friedrich überlässt der neuen Hochschule die ersten zwei Gebäude, in denen in der Ritterstraße das Große Kolleg und in der Petersstraße das Kleine Kolleg untergebracht werden sollten. Am 2. Dezember 1409 ist feierliche Eröffnung im Refektorium des Thomasklosters, in einem Raum, der noch mehr als 100 Jahre als Aula dienen wird. Zugleich wird Johann von Münsterberg zum ersten Rektor gewählt. »Zur Ehre Gottes des Allmächtigen, der ruhmreichen Jungfrau Maria und des ganzen himmlischen Heeres wie auch zum Besten der heiligen Mutter Kirche«, heißt es in der landesherrlichen Gründungsurkunde, »wünschen, bestimmen und verordnen wir, Friedrich der Ältere und Wilhelm, leibliche Brüder, durch Gottes Gunst und Milde Landgrafen von Thüringen, Markgrafen von Meißen und Pfalzgrafen von Sachsen, zu fruchtbarem Fortkommen der Leipziger Universität … dass künftighin an dieser Universität vier Nationen, nämlich Meißner, Sachsen, Bayern und Polen, bestehen sollen …«

Und so haben sie nun eine neue Heimat, nicht nur die aus Prag Ausgezogenen, die nur etwa ein Drittel der insgesamt 369 Studenten und 46 Magistern und Doktoren ausmachen, die im Verzeichnis für das erste Semester festgehalten sind. Historischen Darstellungen zufolge hat der Lehrbetrieb wenig vom

Rektorsiegel zur Beglaubigung von Urkunden.
Seal of the Rector to authenticate documents.

ENDORSEMENT BY THE POPE

Surprisingly, only a short time passed until the actual foundation of Leipzig University. As early as September 1409, Pope Alexander V endorsed the establishment of the Alma mater Lipsiensis, and Margrave Frederick provided the new academia with the first two buildings to house the *Große Kolleg* in *Ritterstraße* and the *Kleine Kolleg* in *Petersstraße.* On 2 December 1409 the festive inauguration took place in the refectory of St. Thomas Monastery, in a room which was to serve as the assembly hall for more than hundred years. At the same time, Johann von Münsterberg was elected to be the first Rector. "In honour of God the Almighty, the glorious Virgin Mary and all of the heavenly host as to the best of our Holy Mother Church", reads the sovereign's charter of foundation, "we, Frederick the Elder and William, natural brothers, by grace and clemency of God, Landgraves of Thuringia, Margraves of Meißen and Counts Palatine of Saxony, wish, determine and order for the fertile advancement of Leipzig University, … that henceforth four nations exist at this university, namely Meißen, Saxon, Bavarian and Polish …"

And thus, those who withdrew from Prague now had a new home. They only accounted for approximately one-third of the 369 students and 46 masters and doctors recorded in the registry for the first ever semester. According to historic descriptions, academic life for the students was far from carefree. First, all students had to complete the so-called Faculty of Arts, where they were taught grammar, logic,

Umzug der deutschen Studenten nach Leipzig, dargestellt auf einer Postkarte von 1909.
Departure of the German students for Leipzig, pictured on a postcard from 1909.

Übergabe der Gründungsurkunde von Friedrich IV. an Rektor Johann von Münsterberg.
Presentation of the foundation charter to Rector Johann von Münsterberg by Frederick IV.

süßen Studentenleben: Zunächst müssen alle Studierenden die so genannte Artistische Fakultät absolvieren, an der sie in Grammatik, Logik, Rhetorik, Arithmetik, Geometrie, Astronomie und Musik Unterricht erhalten. Erst nach Abschluss dieses Grundstudiums können sie an den Fakultäten für Theologie oder Rechtswissenschaft sowie ab 1415 auch an der Medizinischen Fakultät weiterstudieren.

STRENGE REGELN IN BURSEN

Während des Semesters leben die Studenten mit ihren Lehrern in so genannten Bursen zusammen. Die Zeiten sind hart: Da man das Tageslicht voll ausnutzen

rhetoric, arithmetic, geometry, astronomy and music. Only after completing this basic course of study would they have been able to continue their studies at the Faculties of Theology or Law and, from the year 1415 onwards, at the Faculty of Medicine as well.

STRICT RULES IN DORMS

During the semester, students lived together with their teachers in dormitories. Times were tough: daylight was to be used to a maximum, and often courses started as early as five o'clock in the morning. Thereafter the day was divided into prayer and study hours, and doors were closed in the evening at 8 or 9 o'clock.

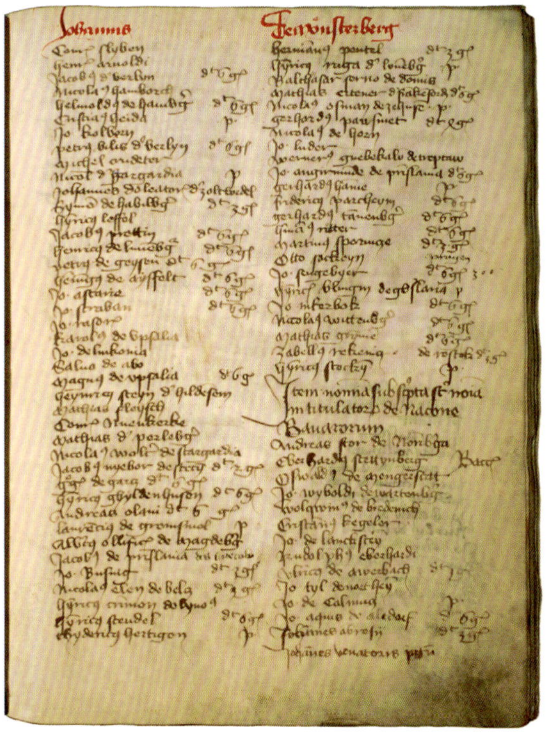

Links: Stammbaum des sächsischen Königshauses mit Erwähnung der Universitätsgründung 1409.
Left: Genealogy of the Saxon Royal Family mentioning the foundation of the University in 1409.

Immatrikulationsliste für das Wintersemester 1409/10.
List of enrolments for the winter semester 1409/10.

Friedrich IV. von Meißen, genannt Friedrich der Streitbare.
Frederick IV of Meißen, also known as Frederick the Belligerent.

Bulle von Papst Alexander V. mit Anweisungen zum Schutz der neuen Universität in Leipzig.
Papal bull of Alexander V with instructions to protect the new Leipzig University.

will, beginnen die Lehrveranstaltungen zum Teil bereits um fünf Uhr morgens, danach teilt sich der Tag in Stunden des Gebets und des Studiums, abends werden die Türen um 20 oder 21 Uhr geschlossen. Es wird Latein gesprochen, alle anderen Sprachen sind verpönt. Zu den Mahlzeiten wird zunächst gebetet, während des Essens dann aus einem theologischen oder anderen wissenschaftlichen Werk vorgelesen.

Wie die studentischen Mahlzeiten aussehen, beschreibt ein Brief aus dem Jahr 1424. Darin äußert sich ein in Leipzig studierender Domherr aus Uppsala zufrieden darüber, dass jedem Studenten ein eigener Becher und eine eigene Schüssel zur Verfügung stünden. Weniger zufriedenstellend scheint aber der Inhalt der Schüsseln. Überliefert ist die Klage über die Eintönigkeit der Kost, in ständiger Wiederholung gibt es Grütze, Suppe, Mus oder Magerfleisch, getrunken wird leichtes Hausbier.

Für den Geschmack der Studierenden viel zu selten stehen ein Braten oder ein Nachtisch auf dem Speisezettel des 15. Jahrhunderts. Und auch die Menge der vorgesetzten Speisen ist offenbar nicht immer ausreichend, in vielfältigen Variationen trösten sich die Studenten damit, dass – wie man auch heute noch weiß – ein voller Bauch nicht gern studiert. Dass es bisweilen knapp zugeht bei Tisch, lässt sich auch an solchen Bursenregeln ablesen, die festlegen, dass die rechtzeitig zum Essen erschienenen Studenten nicht auf Nachzügler warten müssen, sondern deren Portionen mit verzehren dürfen.

Latin was spoken and all other languages were frowned upon. Meals began with a prayer and theological or other scholarly works were read throughout mealtime.

A letter from 1424 described what student meals looked like. A canon from Uppsala studying in Leipzig, was satisfied to state that a personal cup and bowl were available to every student; the content of those bowls, however, seemed to be less satisfying. There have been accounts of complaints regarding the monotony of the menu: a constant diet of porridge, soup, mush or lean meat, and for drink, light home-brewed beer.

According to the students' taste, a roast or dessert were seldom seen on the 15th century menu. And obviously the quantity of dishes served was not sufficient either: the students pacified themselves by saying, in a variety of ways, what is known today as, "you can't work hard on a full stomach". One of the dorm rules suggesting that resources were tight, was that students who arrived on time for the meal did not have to wait for latecomers, but could eat the portions of these tardy students as well.

Die heiligen Brüder Kosmas und Damian als Schutzpatrone der 1415 gegründeten Medizinischen Fakultät.
The Saint Brothers, the twins Cosmas and Damian, and Patron Saints of the Faculty of Medicine, founded in 1415.

Gedenkmünze für Gründer und Förderer Friedrich den Streitbaren.
Commemorative coin for founder and patron Frederick the Belligerent.

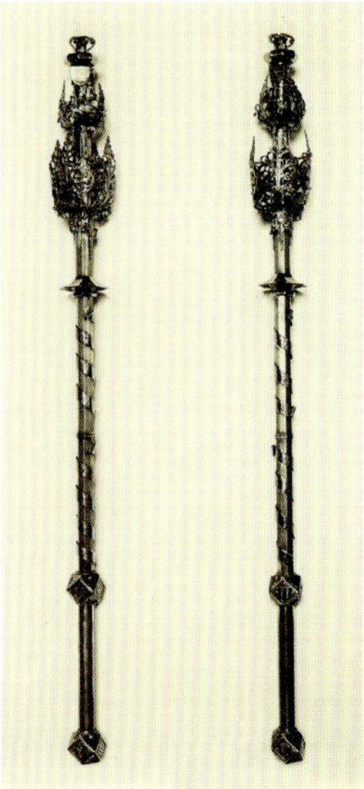

Zepter des Rektors als Zeichen seiner Amtsgewalt.
Sceptre of the Rector as symbol of his authority.

SIEGEL ALS STATUSSYMBOL

In der ständisch geordneten Welt des Mittelalters sind die Baccalaren, Magister und Doktoren als besondere Gruppe leicht zu identifizieren. Zu ihren Merkmalen zählen unter anderem die lateinische Sprache, die Konzentration in wenigen Bereichen innerhalb der Stadtmauern – in Bursen oder Gemeinschaftsquartieren – und die Form der Kleidung mit Mützen, Talaren, Barett oder Birret sowie dem Doktorring. Ihnen verliehene Gerichts-, Steuer- und Zollprivilegien stellen Magister und Doktoren in einigen Belangen gar dem Ritterstand gleich, noch vor dem Adel. Diese Sonderrechte spiegeln sich auch in akademischer Symbolik wider. Das Universitätszepter steht für das akademische Gerichtsprivileg und das Selbstverwaltungsrecht. Neben christlichen Symbolen finden sich auf den Universitätssiegeln auch Bezüge auf weltliche Mächte, wie Stifter oder landesherrliche Regenten, oder Hinweise auf das eigene Lehrgeschäft.

Abgesehen von den Medizinern fehlen bei den Fakultätssiegeln weitgehend Anlehnungen an die Prager Mutteruniversität. Das erhaltene Siegel der Artistenfakultät zeigt beispielsweise im oberen Feld einen älteren Mann, der einen kleinen nackten Knaben auf dem Schoß hält und unterrichtet. Das untere Bild stellt denselben Mann dar, wie er auf einem Katheder sitzt und zwei Studenten lehrt, von denen einer ein Geistlicher zu sein scheint.

BESCHEIDENER ETAT

Nicht gerade auf Rosen gebettet ist die Universität Leipzig im 15. Jahrhundert finanziell. Zwar gibt der Landesherr ihr einen Etat, doch der fällt im Vergleich

SEAL AS STATUS SYMBOL

In the medieval world structered by estates, the bachelors, masters and doctors were easily identified as a particular group. The characteristic traits of this group included knowledge of the Latin language, habitation in a few select areas within the city walls – in dorms or shared accomodation – and similar ways of dress with caps, gowns, beret or biretta as well as the doctor's ring. Court, customs and tax privileges granted to masters and doctors even put them on par with knighthood in some instances, even before nobility. Those special rights were also reflected in the academic symbolism: the University sceptre stands for the academic court privilege and the right of self-government; the University seals carry not only Christian symbols, but also refer to secular powers such as benefactors or territorial rulers or references to proper teaching affairs.

The seals of each of the faculties, except that of Medicine, lack allusion to the Prague mother university. The preserved seal of the Faculty of Arts, for instance, shows in its top half an older man who holds and teaches a small nude boy on his lap. The lower image shows the same man sitting at a lectern teaching two students, one of which seems to be a clergyman.

MODEST BUDGET

In terms of money, the University of Leipzig was anywhere but on a bed of roses in the 15th century. Although the sovereign granted an allocation, this was more than modest compared to his other expenses: in 1471 the grant awarded to the budget equalled only an eighth of the amount spent on his wine-cellar.

Mittelalterliche Pergamenthandschrift in der Universitätsbibliothek.
Medieval parchment manuscript at the University Library.

Der Leidensweg Jesu auf Bildtafeln des Altars der Paulinerkirche, geschaffen von einem unbekannten Künstler um 1500.
Way of the Cross on plates at the altar of Pauliner *Church created by an unknown artist around 1500.*

zu anderen Aufwendungen des Herrschers mehr als bescheiden aus: Im Jahr 1471 liegt der Zuschuss zum Haushalt lediglich bei einem Achtel dessen, was für den fürstlichen Weinkeller ausgegeben wird. Ein festes Gehalt bekommen nur 20 Magister, sodass weitere Gelder aus anderen Quellen fließen müssen. Dazu gehören kirchliche Pfründen, die Zinseinnahmen von Dörfern sowie Studien- und Prüfungsgebühren. Eine weitere Einnahmequelle für die Professoren sind Strafen, die Studenten entrichten müssen, wenn sie schuldhaft gegen die Studienordnung verstoßen.

Zeitgleich mit der Gründung der Universität kommt es in Leipzig zu einer weiteren Neuerung: Die

Only 20 masters drew a fixed salary, so further sources had to be tapped in order to raise funds. These comprised religious benefice, income from interests from villages as well as tuition and examination fees. Students who had culpably infringed study guidelines were subject to fines, which were a further source of income for the professors.

Along with the foundation of the University, Leipzig saw another innovation: the *Löwenapotheke* (Lions Pharmacy) originated as the first and thus oldest pharmacy of the town. The chronicler Johann Jacob Vogel made the connection to the University when writing about the year 1409: “Also in this year, the

Wappen der vier Nationen an der Universität: Sachsen, Meißen, Polen und Bayern.
Crests of the four nations at the University: Saxon, Meißen, Polish and Bavarian.

Löwenapotheke entsteht als erste und damit bis heute älteste Apotheke der Stadt. Den Zusammenhang zur Universität stellt der Chronist Johann Jacob Vogel her, der über das Jahr 1409 schreibt. »Auch sind in diesem Jahr die Apotheken allhier angerichtet worden und ist die zum güldenen Löwen genannte … mit von Prag kommen und ist erstlich ins Eckhaus am Thomasgäßlein, darauf in das Thomasgäßlein und endlich in die Grimmaische Gasse gelegt worden.«

pharmacies have been established here and the one named to the golden lion … come from Prague and was first set in the corner building at *Thomasgäßlein,* then in *Thomasgäßlein* and finally into *Grimmaische Gasse.*”

At that time, Leipzig University had sent its first graduates out into the world. The Faculty of Arts awarded master’s degrees as early as its founding year of 1409. There is documented proof that the costly

Die Leipziger Universität hat zu jener Zeit bereits ihre ersten Absolventen in die Welt verabschiedet. Schon im Gründungsjahr 1409 promoviert die Artistenfakultät Magister, in den höheren Fakultäten finden sich Nachweise über die sehr kostspieligen Doktorpromotionen erst Jahre später.

VIELE REIBEREIEN

Vom geregelten Lehrbetrieb der Neuzeit ist der Unterricht im 15. Jahrhundert weit entfernt. Die dürftige finanzielle Ausstattung der Universität führt dazu, dass besoldete Stellen die Ausnahme sind und zumeist den älteren Lehrenden zufallen, die damit eine angenehme Altersversorgung haben und bisweilen mit dem sicheren Geld in der Tasche Leipzig verlassen. So kann an der Theologischen Fakultät jahrelang keine Prüfung abgenommen werden, weil die entsprechenden Mitglieder der Fakultät nicht zu erreichen sind. Auch der Dekan bildet da keine Ausnahme: Er residiert in Halle. Die Mediziner verdingen sich als Ärzte an den fürstlichen Höfen, und auch die Rechtsgelehrten lassen sich lieber außerhalb der Universität für Beratungen gut bezahlen, anstatt Vorlesungen zu halten.

doctorate programmes were completed in the higher faculties only several years later.

MANY FRICTIONS

Academic life in the 15th century was a far cry from the organised instruction of modern times. The scarce funding the University received made salaried positions the exception. These positions mostly fell to older lecturers, who hence had a comfortable old age provision. Sometimes, after having the money safely in their pockets, they would leave Leipzig. Thus examinations could not be taken at the Faculty of Theology for years, as the respective faculty staff were no longer available. The Dean, who resided in Halle, was no exception either. Physicians hired themselves out to noble courts and also, jurists preferred charging tidy sums for consultations outside of the University instead of lecturing.

Frictions occurred again and again between University members and the town population as well. Although students and masters held intellectual status, they wore secular clothes and weapons, took lodging in the non-latin quarters of Leipzig and wed the

Schwurblatt aus der Matrikel 1409 mit Darstellung des Jüngsten Gerichts.
Oath sheet from the register of 1409 with a depiction of the Last Judgment.

Spätere Darstellung von Geistlichkeit, Studenten und Gefolge des Landesherren zur Gründungszeit.
Later depiction of clergy, students and the sovereign's entourage at the time of the foundation of the University.

Zwischen Universitätsangehörigen und der Stadtbevölkerung kommt es ebenfalls immer wieder zu Reibereien. Die Scholaren und Magister haben zwar einen geistigen Status, tragen jedoch weltliche Kleidung und Waffen, mieten sich in die nichtlateinischen Viertel Leipzigs ein und vermählen sich mit der Bürgerschaft. Besonders bei den bodenständigen Handwerkern sind die Studenten nicht immer wohlgelitten, wie das Beispiel der Leipziger Schusterfehde von 1471 zeigt. In ihrem Groll gegen die Studenten erlassen einige Schusterknechte einen Fehdebrief, es kommt sogar zu bewaffneten Auseinandersetzungen. Aus vielen Quellen ist auch bekannt, dass die Studenten sich immer wieder einen Spaß daraus machen, die üblichen Aufmärsche der Handwerker zu stören.

Die Gratwanderung zwischen akademischer Freiheit und Disziplinierung ist schwierig. Zu viele Freiheiten erzeugen auch in Leipzig immer wieder Gewaltexzesse. Über die unbotmäßigen Studenten der ersten Jahre liegen nur wenige Angaben vor. Zunächst werden ihre Namen einfach nachträglich aus der Matrikel herausradiert. Bis zur Reformation werden von den etwas mehr als 34 000 eingeschriebenen Studenten jedoch nur rund 135 mit einem Universitätsverbot belegt.

Nicht immer sind die Studenten in der Opferrolle zu finden. So weigern sie sich im August 1482 wieder zur mönchischen Tracht zurückzukehren, die Anfang des Jahrhunderts noch das Bild der Universität geprägt

bourgeoisie. Students were not always well regarded, especially by the down-to-earth craftsmen, as the Leipzig cobblers feud showed in 1471: in their grudge against students, some cobblers threw down the gauntlet and there were armed clashes. Many sources reported that students took great pleasure in repeatedly disturbing the traditional craftsmen's parades.

The tightrope walk between academic freedom and disciplinary action was difficult. Too much freedom generated repeated, excessive violence in Leipzig. There are only a few records about the insubordinate students within the first few years after the foundation of the University. Subsequently, their names were simply deleted from the register. Only 135 of the more than 34,000 registered students were imposed with a university ban until the Reformation.

Students found themselves not always in victimhood. In August 1482 they refused to return to monkish dressing, which had shaped the image of

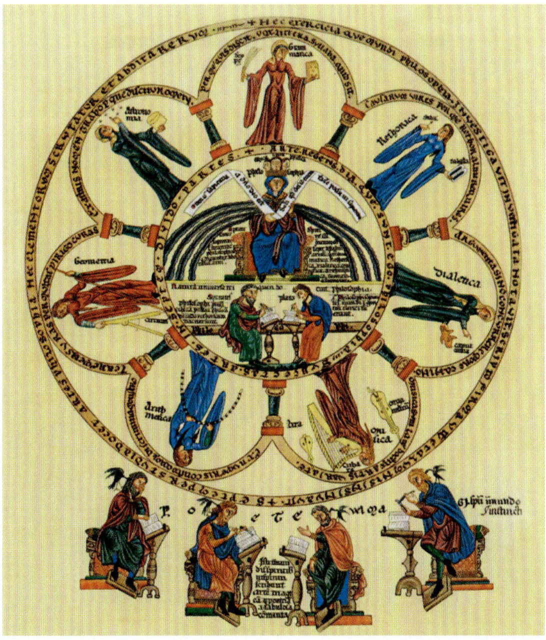

Allegorie auf die »Sieben freien Künste« des Fachbereichs »Artistik«: Grammatik, Rhetorik, Dialektik, Musik, Arithmetik, Geometrie und Astronomie.
Allegory of the seven liberal arts of the Faculty of Arts: grammar, rhetoric, dialectic, music, arithmetic, geometry and astronomy.

Leipziger Stadtansicht mit Grimmaischem Tor und Paulinerkirche (links).
View of the city of Leipzig with Grimmaisches Tor *and* Pauliner *Church (left).*

hatte. Inzwischen sind es die Studenten gewohnt, Hüte mit Federbüschen, bunte Hosen, kurze Mäntel und »gehörnte« Schuhe zu tragen. Einem Erlass des Rektors, diese weltliche Kleidung abzulegen, widersetzen sich die Studenten, es kommt zu Tumulten vor dem Haus des Rektors, sodass der Landesherr mit Landsknechten eingreifen muss.

MONOPOL DES WISSENS FÄLLT

Während in Leipzig mit der Universitätsgründung ein neues Kapitel beginnt, dreht sich die Welt auch außerhalb Sachsens weiter. So etwa in Mainz, wo Johannes Gutenberg 1440 die beweglichen Lettern und damit den modernen Buchdruck erfindet. Mit seiner Entwicklung bricht er das bis dahin bestehende Wissensmonopol der Kirche, die allein in der Lage war, durch die Beschäftigung von Schreibern Bücher zu verbreiten. Am 12. Oktober 1492 und damit kurz vor dem Ende des 15. Jahrhunderts landet schließlich Christoph Columbus auf der Suche nach einer Westpassage nach Indien in einer neuen Welt, die später einmal Amerika heißen wird.

University at the beginning of the century. Meanwhile students got used to wearing tufted hats, coloured pants, short coats and "horned" shoes. The Rector's order to abolish this secular clothing was opposed by the students and brought about riots in front of his house, the sovereign having had to intervene with lansquenets.

KNOWLEDGE MONOPOLY TUMBLED

While the foundation of the University opened a new chapter in Leipzig, the world advanced outside Saxony as well. For instance, in Mainz, where Johannes Gutenberg in 1440 invented movable type and thus modern printing. With his invention he broke up the knowledge monopoly of the church. Up to that date, the church was solely able to distribute books, the reproduction of which was made possible by the employment of scribes. Finally, on 12 October 1492 and thus near the end of the 15th century, Christopher Columbus, in his search for a westward route to the Indies, landed in a new world, which would later be called America.

DAS 15. JAHRHUNDERT
THE 15TH CENTURY

BLICK IN DIE WELT
VIEW OF THE WORLD

1410 Polnisch-litauische Truppen besiegen in der Schlacht von Tannenberg den Deutschen Orden. Polish-Lithuanian troops defeat the Teutonic Order in the Battle of Tannenberg.

1421 Kaiser Yongle erklärt Peking zur Hauptstadt der Ming-Dynastie. The Yongle Emperor declares Beijing the capital of the Ming Dynasty.

1429 Jeanne d'Arc befreit das französische Orléans von den englischen Belagerern. Joan of Arc liberates the French city of Orléans from English besiegers.

1440 Nicolaus Cusanus erklärt das Universum für unendlich. Nicholas of Kues declares the universe to be infinite.

1452 Johannes Gutenberg druckt erstmals mit beweglichen Bleilettern die Bibel. Johannes Gutenberg prints the Bible using movable lead type for the first time.

1453 Die Türken erobern Konstantinopel und besiegeln das Ende von Byzanz. The Turks conquer Constantinople and thus seal the fate of Byzantium.

1469 Isabella von Kastilien und Ferdinand II. von Aragón begründen mit ihrer Hochzeit den neuen Gesamtstaat Spanien. Isabella of Castile and Ferdinand II of Aragón, by their marriage, establish the new and unified state of Spain.

1480 Iwan III. beendet die Mongolenherrschaft in Russland. Iwan III ends Mongol domination of Russia.

1484 Papst Innozenz VIII. legitimiert mit einer Bulle die Hexenverfolgung. Pope Innocent VIII, in a papal bull, legitimizes the prosecution of witches.

1485 Die Schlacht von Bosworth leitet das Ende der langjährigen Rosenkriege in England ein. The Battle of Bosworth Field heralds the end of the long lasting Wars of the Roses in England.

1492 Christoph Columbus landet an der Küste von Amerika. Christopher Columbus lands on the coast of America.

1495 Der erste größere Syphilis-Ausbruch in Neapel entwickelt sich zu einer Epidemie in Europa. The first great outbreak of syphilis in Naples developes into an epidemic in Europe.

1498 Der Portugiese Vasco da Gama erreicht Indien erstmals auf dem Seeweg. The Portuguese Vasco da Gama reaches India by sea for the first time.

BERÜHMTHEITEN AN DER UNIVERSITÄT
ILLUSTRIOUS PEOPLE AT THE UNIVERSITY

Johannes Otto ca. 1360 – 1416
Theologe, 1398 Rektor der Karlsuniversität Prag, 1409 Gründungsrektor der Universität Leipzig, nach seinem Geburtsort auch Johann von Münsterberg genannt. Theologian, 1398 Rector of Charles University in Prague, 1409 Founding Rector of Leipzig University, also, named after his birthplace, Johann von Münsterberg.

Conrad Celtis 1459 – 1508
Humanist und Dichter, hält ab 1486 in Leipzig Vorlesungen zur Poetik, wird 1487 als erster Deutscher von Kaiser Friedrich III. als »Poeta laureatus« gekrönt. Humanist and poet, lectured in poetics in Leipzig from 1486, first German to be crowned "Poet Laureate" by the German Emperor Frederick III.

Heinrich Stromer 1482 – 1542
Arzt und Gründer des weltberühmten Lokals »Auerbachs Keller«, ab 1497 Studium, dann Magister, Doktor der Medizin, Professor für Pathologie und Rektor. Physician and founder of the world-famous restaurant "Auerbachs Keller", from 1497 study, then Magister, Doctor of Medicine, Professor of Pathology and Rector.

Konrad Wimpina ca. 1460 – 1531
Katholischer Theologe, ab 1479 Studium in Leipzig, Lehrtätigkeit als Magister und Professor, 1494 Rektor, 1506 Gründungsrektor der Universität Frankfurt/Oder. Catholic theologian, from 1479 study in Leipzig, taught as Magister and Professor, 1494 Rector, 1506 Founding Rector of the University of Frankfurt/Oder.

Martin Schongauer ca. 1450 – 1491
Maler und Grafiker, erstmals urkundlich erfasst durch Einschreibung 1465 an der Universität Leipzig, beeinflusst mit seiner Kunst Michelangelo und Dürer. Painter and graphic artist, first documented in the registration record at the University of Leipzig in 1465. His art influenced Michelangelo and Dürer.

NIEDERGANG, ERSTE HOCHSCHULREFORM UND UNERWARTETER REICHTUM
DECLINE, FIRST UNIVERSITY REFORM AND UNEXPECTED WEALTH

Ab 1502 entsteht harte Konkurrenz für Leipzig – die neue Universität in Wittenberg, kaum zwei Tagesreisen entfernt. Der Neugründung geht die Teilung des Kurfürstentums Sachsen-Wittenberg in den ernestinischen und albertinischen Herrschaftsbereich voraus. Diese Aufteilung hat wesentlichen Einfluss auf die Entwicklung der Leipziger Universität. Während Kurfürst Friedrich der Weise im ernestinischen Teil den Reformator Martin Luther tatkräftig unterstützt und ihn an die neu gegründete Universität Wittenberg beruft, ist der im albertinischen Teil herrschende Herzog Georg der Bärtige ein ausgesprochener Gegner der Reformation.

Der neue Geist an der Wittenberger Universität macht diese auch für Leipziger Studenten überaus attraktiv. Obwohl Herzog Georg es ausdrücklich verbietet, wechselt eine ganz Reihe von ihnen nach Wittenberg. Strafandrohungen können sie nicht von diesem Schritt abhalten, wobei sicher nicht nur konfessionelle, sondern auch wirtschaftliche Gründe eine Rolle spielen. Denn Leipzig erlebt Anfang des 16. Jahrhunderts einen wirtschaftlichen Aufschwung: durch den erblühenden Buchdruck, dem damit verbundenen Handel und die Beteiligung der Stadt am Silberbergbau in Schneeberg. Das spült viel Geld in die Stadt, was wiederum dazu führt, dass die Lebenshaltungskosten deutlich höher sind als im eher beschaulichen Wittenberg.

The newly founded university in Wittenberg, hardly a two day journey from Leipzig, provided fierce competition for the University of Leipzig from 1502. This new foundation was preceded by the division of the Electorate of Saxe-Wittenberg into the Ernestine and Albertine domains. This division had essential influence on the development of the University of Leipzig. In the Ernestine domain, Frederick the Wise, Elector of Saxony, actively supported Martin Luther and appointed him to the new University of Wittenberg. George the Bearded, Duke of Saxony and ruler in the Albertine domain however, was a pronounced opponent of the Reformation.

The new spirit at the University of Wittenberg made it extremely attractive to students from Leipzig as well. Although Duke George the Bearded explicitly prohibited it, a whole number of them enrolled in Wittenberg. Threats of punishment could not prevent them from taking this step, while not only denominational, but also economic reasons played a role: Leipzig experienced an economic revival at the beginning of the 16th century through the blossoming printing industry and the accompanying trade; and the city's involvement in silver mining in Schneeberg. All this injected a lot of money into the city, and as a result, living expenses were considerably higher than in the rather quiet Wittenberg.

Siegel der Theologischen Fakultät.
Seal of the Faculty of Theology.

Auf Holz gemaltes Wappenbild der Bayerischen Landsmannschaft an der Leipziger Universität.
Crest of the Bavarian Student Corporation at the University of Leipzig, painted on wood.

Turmuhr am 1557 eingeweihten Alten Rathaus.
Turret clock at the Old City Hall, inaugurated in 1557.

SELBSTBEWUSSTES HANDWERK

Seit Gründung der Leipziger Universität hatte es immer wieder Auseinandersetzungen mit den Handwerksgesellen in der Stadt gegeben. Vor allem Schuster und Kürschner greifen die Studenten an. Für sie sind insbesondere zur Fastnachtszeit Leipzigs Straßen kein gutes Pflaster: Sie sehen sich den Handwerksgesellen gegenüber, die sich durch den Rat der Stadt höher gestellt fühlen und äußerst selbstbewusst auftreten. Der Fastnachtstanz im Rathaus zum Beispiel war bis zum 16. Jahrhundert nur Adligen, wohlhabenden Bürgern und Beamten des Landesherrn vorbehalten. Die Zünfte aber erlangen wachsende Bedeutung, und so wird dem »ehrlich Handwerk« nun auch der Zutritt zum Tanzvergnügen gewährt. Für die Stadt hat diese Zulassung interessante finanzielle Konsequenzen: Die Handwerker bringen ihre Rundtänze mit, mit denen sie die »artigen Schritttänze« bedrohen. Schließlich werden die flotten Rundtänze verboten, da sie gegen die guten Sitten verstoßen, denn es kommt vor, dass sich »ein Weibsperson so gedrehet, daß sie darob gar entblößt ward«. Das Verbot lässt sich aber nicht durchsetzen, und schließlich kommt der Rat der Stadt auf die Idee, durch Einführung einer Rundtanzgebühr vom lockeren Treiben zu profitieren.

Die Obrigkeit fürchtet die Fastnachtszeit, da es immer wieder zu Massenschlägereien zwischen Studenten

SELF-CONFIDENT TRADE

There had been repeated conflicts with the journeymen in town since the foundation of the University. Mainly cobblers and furriers attacked the students. The streets of Leipzig were not a good place to be for the latter, especially during Shrovetide; they found themselves face to face with journeymen who considered themselves to be of a higher rank, thanks to the City Council. These journeymen were very self-confident. The Shrovetide Dance in the townhall, for instance, used to be reserved for nobility, wealthy citizens and public servants of the sovereign until the 16th century. Guilds, however, grew in importance and thus the "honest tradesmen" were now granted access to the dance as well. This held interesting financial implications for the city. The tradesmen brought their round dances along, by which they challenged the "well-behaved step dance". Finally, the brisk round dances were banned as they infringed upon morality, for it happened that "a female turned so much that she even exposed herself". The ban was not enforceable and this is what finally gave the City Council the idea to introduce a round dance fee, in order to benefit from the misstep.

Authorities feared the Shrovetide as there were repeated punchfests between students and journeymen: in 1521, for instance, bloody clashes were recorded. In

Prachtvoll gestaltete Matrikel von 1595.
Magnificently designed students' register from 1595.

Leipzig im Jahr 1572 mit der Moritzbastei (Mitte).
Leipzig and the Moritzbastei *(centre) in 1572.*

und Handwerksgesellen kommt: 1521 beispielsweise werden blutige Zusammenstöße verzeichnet. 1533 führen die Tumulte sogar zum Sturm auf die Kollegiengebäude der Universität. Auch 1588 weiß die Chronik von einer »großen Schlägerei auf dem Markte zwischen Studenten und Schuhknechten« zu berichten. 1545 werden innerhalb eines Semesters allein drei Totschlagsdelikte und zahlreiche andere Übergriffe gegen Studenten registriert. Als sich der Rektor beim Rat der Stadt beschwert, reagiert dieser mit den lapidaren Worten: »Es müssen die euren stetts recht haben.«

RITUAL ZUR AUFNAHME

Rektor Heinrich Stromer von Auerbach, Besitzer des später durch Goethes »Faust« weltweit bekannten Lokals »Auerbachs Keller«, gelingt es 1531, Herzog Georg von der Einrichtung einer Professur für Physiologie an der Medizinischen Fakultät zu überzeugen. Zehn Jahre später kommen eine Professur für Anatomie und Chirurgie hinzu. Es mag sein, dass diese neuen Angebote auch neue Studenten nach Leipzig ziehen. Sicher ist, dass die Studienanfänger sich der Deposition unterziehen müssen, einem Ritual zur Immatrikulation. Sie gelten bis zum Eintritt in die Universität als unzivilisiert, als »Wildtiere«. Dementsprechend werden sie zur Deposition auch ausstaffiert: mit großen Hörnern und Eberzähnen, die mit grotesken, riesigen Instrumenten entfernt werden. Das Kopfhaar und der Bart werden getrimmt, die Ohren sauber gemacht und der Körper »gehobelt« – ein »ungehobelter Kerl« kann

Epitaph von Rektor und Universitätsreformer Caspar Borner.
Epitaph of Rector and University reformer Caspar Borner.

1533, the riots even led to an attack on the collegia buildings of the University. Also, in 1588, the chronicle reported a "brawl between students and cobblers in the market". Three instances of manslaughter and numerous other assaults against students were recorded within only one semester in 1545. When the Rector complained to the City Council, he was given the lapidary answer "Yours' must be always right."

INITIATION RITUAL

Rector Heinrich Stromer von Auerbach, owner of the wine bar, "Auerbachs Keller", that would later become world famous thanks to Goethe's "Faust", successfully convinced Duke George to set up a Chair of Physiology at the Faculty of Medicine in 1531. Ten years later, Chairs of Anatomy and Surgery were added. Perhaps these offers attracted new students to Leipzig as well. One thing is certain: freshmen had to undergo deposition, an initiation ritual for enrolment. They were regarded as uncivilized, as "wild animals", until entry into university. They were equipped accordingly with huge horns and boar's teeth, which were removed using bizarre and giant instruments. Hair and beard were trimmed, ears were cleaned and the body was "polished" – hence a "rough customer" could not have been a student. Finally, the "salt of wisdom" was stuffed into the students' mouths and the "wine of joy" was poured over their heads. They

Rechts: Der 1528 bis 1538 von Heinrich Stromer errichtete Auerbachs Hof mit Weinausschank im Keller.
Right: Auerbachs Hof *with wine cellar, erected by Heinrich Stromer from 1528 to 1538.*

Matrikel von 1508 unter Rektor Heinrich Stromer von Auerbach.
Students' register of 1508 under Rector Heinrich Stromer von Auerbach.

deshalb kein Student gewesen sein. Schließlich werden den Studenten das »Salz der Weisheit« in den Mund gestopft und der »Wein der Freude« über den Kopf geschüttet. Und für die ganze Prozedur müssen sie auch noch eine Gebühr entrichten. Die Leipziger Universität ist deutschlandweit die einzige Hochschule, die bei der Deposition verwendete Instrumente noch heute in ihrer Sammlung hat.

Dass diese »Zivilisierung« nicht immer den gewünschten Erfolg hat, geht aus den Rektoratsakten, den Acta Rectorum, hervor. Darin werden zahlreiche Fälle aufgeführt, in denen Studenten Mädchen eine Entschädigung zahlen müssen, nachdem sie diese verführt haben. Geklagt wird auch darüber, dass die Studenten Dirnen in ihre Wohnungen mitnehmen. Bordellbetreiberinnen beschweren sich darüber, dass die Studiosi weder ihr Bier, noch die ihnen geleisteten Dienste bezahlen. Gern stören die Studenten zudem Feste der Bürger, wobei das Eindringen in Hochzeitsfeierlichkeiten besonders beliebt gewesen sein muss. Schließlich wird sogar davon berichtet, dass 1567 vier Studenten einen Apotheker festgehalten und Geld erpresst haben. Bei der Geldübergabe wird einer der Erpresser gefasst – und zum Tode verurteilt.

STUDENT MIT NEUN JAHREN

Leider steht nicht geschrieben, wie alt der Delinquent bei seiner Enthauptung war. Bekannt ist jedoch, dass die Altersstruktur der Leipziger Studentenschaft im 16. Jahrhundert eine erhebliche Spreizung aufweist. Es kommt häufig vor, dass sich auch ältere Männer einem

were even charged a fee for the whole procedure. Leipzig University is the only one throughout Germany to have instruments that were used for deposition in its collection to this day.

The Acta Rectorum, the files from the Rector's office, unveil that this "civilizing" procedure was not always fruitful. Therein numerous cases were listed where students had to pay a compensation to girls after having seduced them. There were also complaints about students taking strumpets into their apartments. Madams of brothels complained that students paid neither for their beer nor for the services rendered. The students voluntarily disrupted the festivities of the citizens, the intrusion into wedding receptions having been especially popular. There were records of four students having detained and blackmailed a pharmacist in 1567. When one of the blackmailers wanted to collect the money he was seized and sentenced to death.

Matrikelbuch vom Wintersemester 1505 mit heiliger Katharina, Schutzpatronin der Theologen, Philosophen und Advokaten.
Book of registers from the winter semester of 1505 showing Saint Catherine, patron saint of theologians, philosophers and advocates.

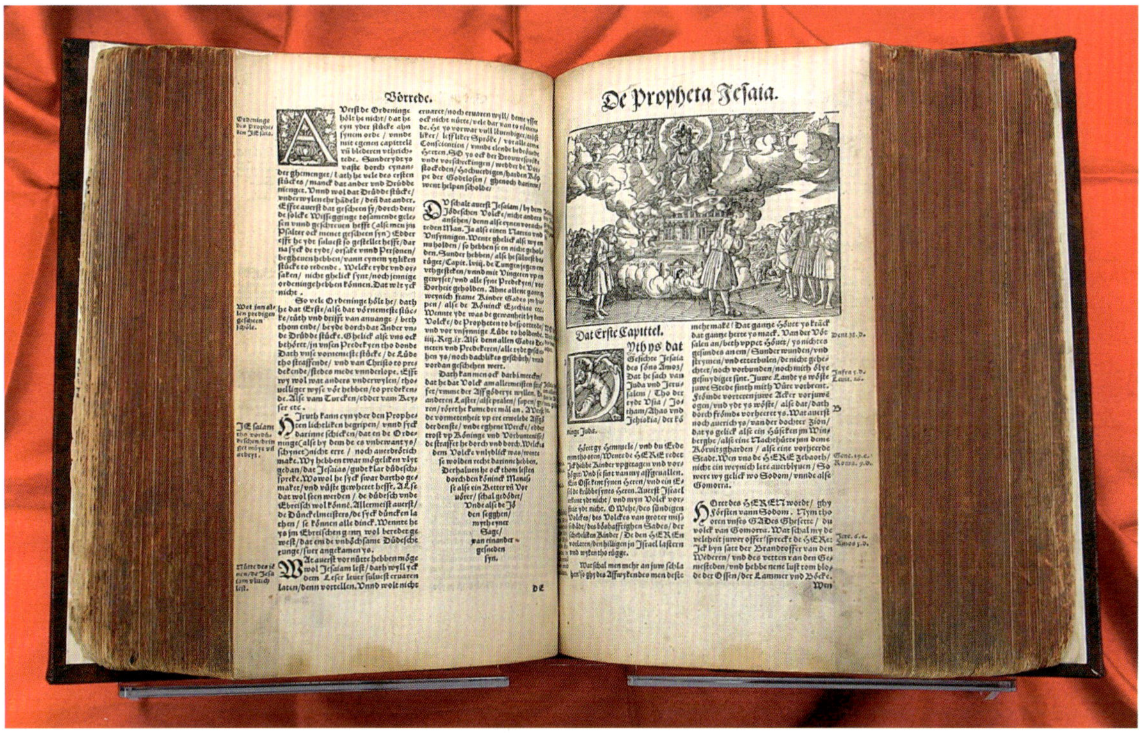

Original Luther-Bibel aus dem Jahr 1545.
Original Luther Bible from 1545.

Studium widmen, wenn sie die nötigen Mittel dazu erlangen können. Insbesondere bei der Geistlichkeit ist das Studieren beliebt – entbindet es doch mitunter mehrere Jahre von der Residenzpflicht. Andererseits gibt es Studenten, die bereits in jungen Jahren an der Universität eingeschrieben sind. Ihr jugendliches Alter und die zum Teil geringe schulische Vorbildung erfordern es, dass die Universität erst einmal Grundlagen vermitteln muss. So stehen Latein und Mathematik auf dem Lehrplan – und zwar für Anfänger.

Einer der jüngsten Leipziger Studenten dürfte Georg Kleinschmidt gewesen sein. Am 10. Juni 1498 geboren, wird er schon 1507 an der Alma mater Lipsiensis aufgenommen – im zarten Alter von gerade einmal neun Jahren. Kleinschmidt, auch Kleynschmidt geschrieben, der später unter dem Namen Georg Curio von Martin Luther als Arzt sehr geschätzt wird, ist nicht etwa ein Wunderkind, das sich innerhalb kürzester Zeit Wissen aneignet. Sieben Jahre dauert es, bis er das Baccalaurat abschließt. Magister der Philosophie wird er im Dezember 1522. Nach seinem Wechsel in die Medizin im Jahr 1527 dauert es weitere vier Jahre bis er den Doktortitel erhält – im italienischen Padua zwar, aber er kehrt vorübergehend nach Leipzig zurück, bevor er an der Universität Wittenberg zu wissenschaftlichem Ruhm gelangt.

DURCHBRUCH DER REFORMATION

Zu jenem Zeitpunkt sind die Wittenberger den Leipzigern in der Attraktivität noch immer voraus, denn erst nach dem Tod Georg des Bärtigen kann sich die Reformation auch an der Pleiße durchsetzen. Georg stand Luther zunächst durchaus positiv gegenüber

STUDENT AT THE AGE OF NINE

Unfortunately, there is no record of the age at which the delinquent was decapitated. It is known, however, that the student body in Leipzig featured a wide distribution in age during the 16th century. It often happened, that older men applied themselves to studies, if they could find the necessary means. Studying was particularly popular among members of the clergy, as sometimes it released them from the obligation of retaining a residence for several years. On the other hand, there were students who were already registered at the University at a younger age. Their youth and somewhat insufficient educational background required the University to teach them the fundamentals first. The curriculum featured Latin and mathematics for beginners.

Georg Kleinschmidt might have been one of the youngest students in Leipzig. Born on 10 June 1498, he was admitted to the Alma mater Lipsiensis as early as 1507 at the tender age of nine. Kleinschmidt, also spelled Kleynschmidt, would later become much appreciated by Martin Luther as a physician under the name Georg Curio. He was by no means a wunderkind who acquired knowledge within an incredibly short time. He took seven years to complete his Bachelor's degree. He became Master of Philosophy in December 1522. After he changed his field of study to medicine in 1527, it took four more years until he received his doctorate – indeed in the Italian city of Padua, but he temporarily returned to Leipzig before acquiring scientific and academic renown at the University of Wittenberg.

Hauszeichen an »Auerbachs Keller« von 1530.
House sign at "Auerbachs Keller" from 1530.

Spottrelief mit Papst, Kaiser und Reformator.
Satirical relief with Pope, Emperor and Reformer.

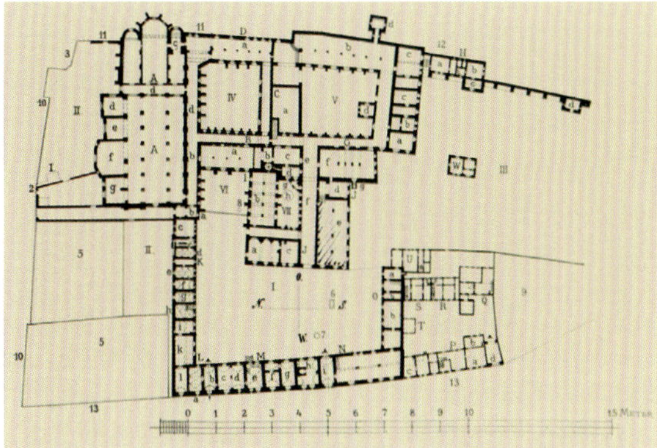

Links: Grundriss des Paulinums um 1550.
Left: Layout of the Paulinum circa 1550.

Stadtansicht mit Universitätsgebäuden 1547.
View of the city and the University's buildings in 1547.

und interessierte sich für dessen Ideen einer Reformation der Kirche. Nach der Disputation von Leipzig im Jahr 1519, die der katholische Johannes Eck mit Martin Luther, Andreas Karlstadt und Philipp Melanchthon als führenden Vertretern der Reformation führt, wird Herzog Georg jedoch zum erbitterten Gegner des Reformators, auch wenn das kirchengeschichtlich bedeutende Streitgespräch ohne Sieger und Verlierer endet. Noch heute ist im Hof des Fregehauses in der Katharinenstraße ein Relief von 1535 zu sehen, das Luther verspottet: Papst und Kaiser stehen sich vertraut gegenüber, der Reformator liegt unter ihnen am Boden.

Doch schon vier Jahre später, Georg stirbt 1539, übernimmt dessen jüngerer Bruder Heinrich der Fromme die Nachfolge. Er ist ein erklärter Anhänger Luthers und setzt sich die Einführung der Reformation auch im albertinischen Sachsen zum Ziel. Schon zu Pfingsten 1539 darf der Reformator in der Thomaskirche predigen. Auch die Universität profitiert davon.

THE BREAKTHROUGH OF REFORMATION

At the time, Wittenberg still outpaced Leipzig as an alluring place to be. For Reformation could only be established at the *Pleiße* river after George the Bearded had died. At first, George was quite sympathetic to Luther and took an interest in his ideas for a reformation of the church. However, Duke George turned into a virulent opponent of the Reformation following the Leipzig Debate in 1519, even though it ended without a winner or loser. The debate was led by the Catholic Johannes Eck and by Martin Luther, Andreas Karlstadt and Philipp Melanchthon, the leading proponents of Reformation; and would have an impact on church history. Until this day, a 1535 relief in the court of *Fregehaus* in *Katharinenstraße* mocks Luther: the Pope and Emperor, in a familiar manner, facing each other, whereas the Reformer is depicted beneath them on the ground.

Four years later, in 1539, George passed away. His younger brother Henry the Pious, who was a professed

Links: Reformator Martin Luther, Prediger in der Universitätskirche 1545.
Left: Reformer Martin Luther, preacher at the University Church in 1545.

»Die Heroen der Naturwissenschaft« aus dem Gemälde »Das Zeitalter der Reformation«.
"The heros of the natural sciences" from the painting "The Era of Reformation".

Instrumente für das Aufnahmeritual der Studienanfänger.
Instruments for the initiation ritual for first-year students.

Allerdings dauert es noch eine Weile, bevor sich Strukturen und Verhältnisse ändern. Neben dem Problem der schlechten geistigen Verfassung der Universität verzögert auch der Mangel an Geld die Reform. Zwei Männer ebnen ihr dann doch den Weg: Caspar Borner, ab Herbst 1539 neuer Rektor, und Herzog Moritz, der 1541 seinen Vater beerbt. Borner liefert gemeinsam mit dem Humanisten Philipp Melanchthon und dem Universitätsreformer Joachim Camerarius die Ideen und kämpft für deren Umsetzung. Und eine Dotation von Herzog Moritz verschafft der Universität schließlich auch den nötigen finanziellen Spielraum dafür. »Ich will mich dermaßen gegen die Universität erzeigen, daß jedermann spüren soll, daß sie mir lieb sei«, verkündet er. Emil Friedberg schreibt in seiner Universitätsgeschichte von 1898: »Die Dotation war über Erwarten groß. Sie machte Leipzig mit einem Schlage zur reichsten Universität Deutschlands.«

supporter of Luther, succeeded him. Henry set himself the target of introducing Reformation in Albertine Saxony as well. In 1539, at the time of Whitsun, the Reformer was allowed to preach in St. Thomas Church. The University benefited from this new development as well. It would be a while before structures and circumstances changed. Besides the insufficient intellectual capital at the University, the shortage of money delayed reform as well. Two men did pave the way for reform though: Caspar Borner, the new Rector from autumn 1539, and Duke Maurice, who succeeded his father in 1541. Borner furnished, along with humanist Philipp Melanchthon and University reformer Joachim Camerarius, the ideas and fought for their implementation. An endowment by Duke Maurice provided the University with the required financial scope. "I want to behave toward the university in a way that everybody shall feel I treasure it," he announced. Emil Friedberg wrote in his University history of 1898: "The donation was huge beyond expectation. It made Leipzig the richest university of Germany in a single stroke."

Moritz von Sachsen, Förderer der Universität.
Maurice of Saxony, supporter of the University.

Rechts: Das zwischen 1503 und 1513 errichtete Neue Kolleg, später Rotes Kolleg genannt, in der Ritterstraße.
Right: Neues Kolleg *on* Ritterstraße, *erected between 1503 and 1513, later named* Rotes Kolleg.

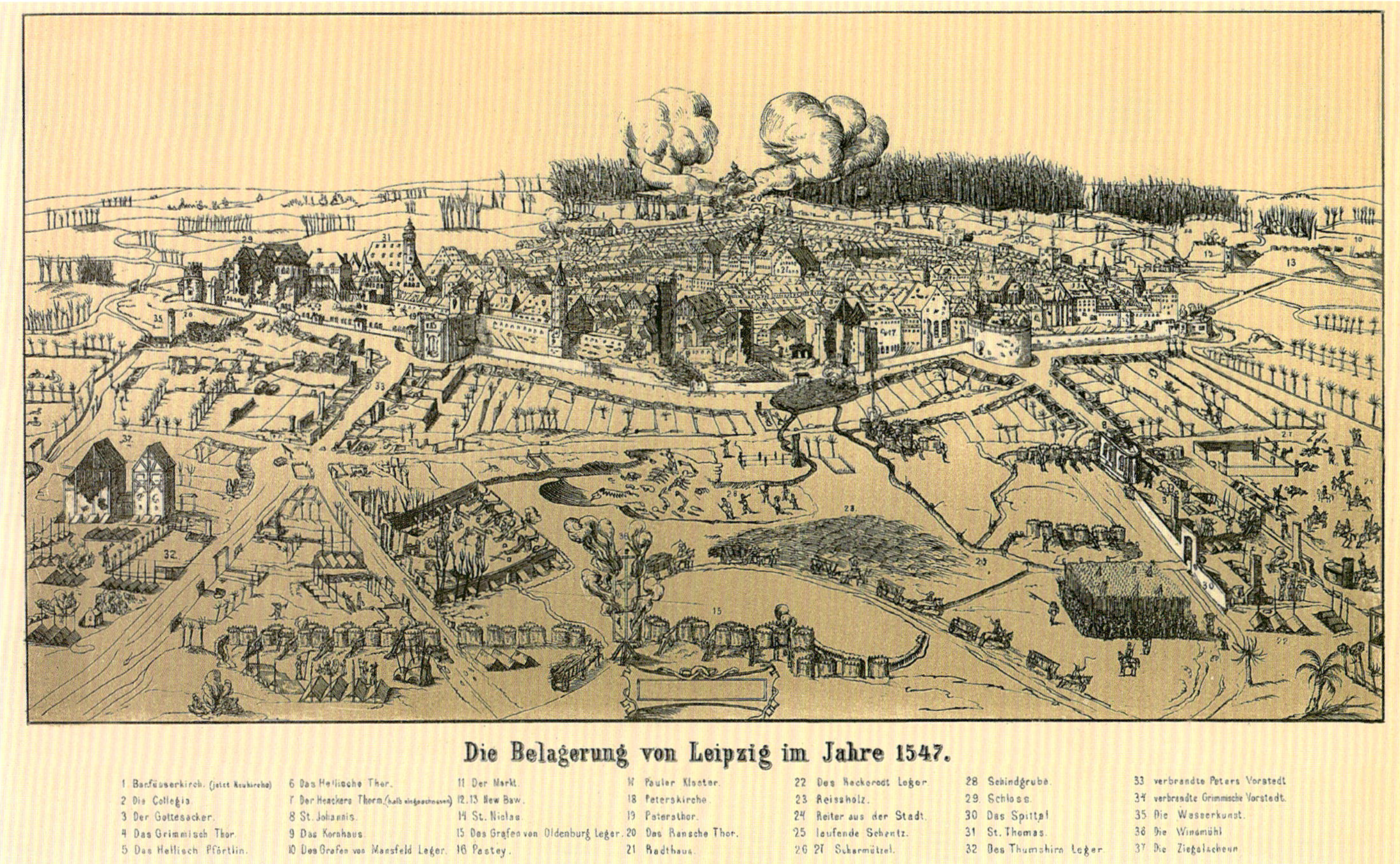

Belagerung der Stadt im Schmalkaldischen Krieg.
Siege of the city during the Schmalkaldic War.

EIGENER CAMPUS

2 000 Goldgulden jährlich verheißt Herzog Moritz. Außerdem übereignet er der Hochschule den umfangreichen Gebäudekomplex des Dominikanerklosters St. Pauli. Die Universität übernimmt das verlassene und geplünderte Gelände zunächst mit erheblichem Bauaufwand. Bis dato waren die Gebäude der Hochschule innerhalb der Stadtmauern verstreut, nun entsteht ein Campus, der zahlreiche Annehmlichkeiten bietet. Neben dem Bibliothekssaal, zwei Versammlungssälen – einem Sommer- und einem Winterrefektorium – verfügt die Universität nun über Klostergarten mit Krankenstube, Apothekergewölbe, Destillierhaus, Brauhaus, Schneiderei, Schusterei, Schweine-, Rinder- und Pferdeställe, Malzhaus, Backstube, Weinkeller, Bad und Küchentrakt.

Auch inhaltlich wird der Niedergang der Universität gestoppt. Rektor Borner gelingt es, zumeist aus säkularisierten Klöstern die Bibliotheken zu erwerben: rund 4 000 Bände und 1 500 Handschriften. Die Medizinische Fakultät bekommt eine Professur für Anatomie. Die Philosophen müssen den halbjährlichen Wechsel der Vorlesungsgebiete, die so genannten »walzenden Lektionen«, aufgeben: Feste Professuren entstehen. Außerdem werden neue Professuren für Sprachen, höhere Mathematik und Geschichte der Philosophie eingerichtet. Auch die Reformation der Theologischen Fakultät findet ihren Abschluss: Sichtlicher Ausdruck dafür ist die Weihe

THE UNIVERSITY'S OWN CAMPUS

Duke Maurice promised 2,000 Guilders annually. Furthermore, he gifted the University with a comprehensive complex of buildings of the Dominican monastery, St. Pauli. The University first took over the abandoned and pillaged premises which required substantial reconstruction expenditures. The university buildings had been scattered throughout the city until the creation of a single campus, which offered numerous conveniences. Besides a library, there were two assembly rooms – one summer and one winter refectory. The University disposed of the monastery garden which included an infirmary, pharmacy, distillery, brewery, tailor's shop, cobbler's shop, pigsty, cowshed and horse barn, oast-house, bakery, wine cellar, bathroom and kitchen facilities.

The intellectual decline of the University was halted as Rector Borner successfully acquired libraries, mostly from secularized monasteries: about 4,000 volumes and 1,500 manuscripts. The Faculty of Medicine was given a Chair of Anatomy. Philosophers had to give up the biannual rotation of lecture topics, the so-called "rolling lessons", and permanent chairs emerged. Furthermore, new Chairs of Languages, Higher Mathematics, and History of Philosophy were established. The reformation of the Faculty of Theology was completed as well, the visible expression of which was the consecration of the *Pauliner* Church to become the University Church St. Pauli, where

Lutherischer Theologe, Professor und Superintendent Nikolaus Selnecker.
Lutheran theologian, professor and superintendent Nikolaus Selnecker.

Studentische Trachten aus dem 16., 17. und 18. Jahrhundert.
Student costumes from the 16th, 17th and 18th centuries.

der Paulinerkirche zur Universitätskirche St. Pauli, in der Reformator Martin Luther am 12. August 1545 eine Predigt hält.

Mit der früheren Klosterkirche hat die Hochschule zudem einen Raum, den sie für Promotionen und akademische Feiern nutzen kann. Auch Predigten werden gehalten – wenngleich der Rat der Stadt, der selbst auf die Übernahme des Klosterkomplexes gehofft hatte, erklärt: Die Universität könne in der Kirche »tanzen lassen, nicht aber predigen«.

the Reformer Martin Luther preached the sermon on 12 August 1545.

Having acquired the former monastery church, the University now owned a facility that could be used for graduation ceremonies where doctorates were conferred, and other academic functions. Sermons were delivered there as well – although the City Council, which had also hoped to take over the monastery buildings, declared the University "could have people dance in the church, but not preach".

»Christus als Erlöser« mit Johannes dem Täufer, Lukas Cranach und Martin Luther auf einem Cranach-Gemälde von 1555.
"Christ as the Redeemer", with John the Baptist, Lucas Cranach and Martin Luther in a Cranach painting from 1555.

Rechts: Papst Leo X. bestätigt 1514 das kaiserliche Messeprivileg für Leipzig.
Right: Pope Leo X confirms the imperial trade fair privilege for Leipzig in 1514.

DAS 16. JAHRHUNDERT
THE 16TH CENTURY

BLICK IN DIE WELT
VIEW OF THE WORLD

1501 Franz von Taxis beginnt mit dem Aufbau des Postwesens in Europa. Franz von Taxis starts the establishment of a postal service in Europe.

1502 Bauern und Bürger um Joß Fritz erheben sich im Bundschuh-Aufstand gegen den Adel. Peasants and townsfolk rise with Joss Fritz against nobility in the Bundschuh rebellion.

1503 Leonardo da Vinci malt die Mona Lisa. Leonardo da Vinci paints the Mona Lisa.

1509 In Konstantinopel sterben bei einem großen Erdbeben 13 000 Menschen. 13,000 people die in a devastating earthquake in Constantinople.

1513 Niccoló Macchiavelli beschreibt in seinen Schriften die Macht als Grundlage des Staates. Niccoló Macchiavelli decribes, in his writings, power as the basis of the state.

1514 Der Aufstieg der Fugger zur europäischen Handelsmacht mit politischem Einfluss beginnt. The Fugger family rises to become a European commercial power with political influence.

1515 Die Schweiz proklamiert nach der verlorenen Schlacht bei Marignano ihre Neutralität. Switzerland proclaims its neutrality after losing the Battle of Marignano.

1517 Martin Luther setzt mit seinem Thesenanschlag zu Wittenberg die Reformation in Gang. Martin Luther sparks the Reformation by displaying his Theses in Wittenberg.

1519 Der spanische Eroberer Hernando Cortés unterwirft in Mexiko das Aztekenreich. The Spanish Conquerer Hernán Cortés subdues the Aztec empire in Mexico.

1525 Der Bauernkrieg gegen Adel und Geistlichkeit fordert 100 000 Menschenleben. The Peasants' War against gentry and clergy claims 100,000 lives.

1543 Nikolaus Kopernikus veröffentlicht sein heliozentrisches Weltsystem. Nicolaus Copernicus publishes his heliocentric system.

1582 Papst Gregor XIII. führt den gregorianischen Kalender mit Schaltjahr ein. Pope Gregor XIII introduces the Gregorian calendar which includes the leap year.

1595 William Shakespeare schreibt »Romeo und Julia«. William Shakespeare writes "Romeo and Juliet".

BERÜHMTHEITEN AN DER UNIVERSITÄT
ILLUSTRIOUS PEOPLE AT THE UNIVERSITY

Thomas Müntzer 1489–1525
Evangelischer Theologe und Sozialrevolutionär in der Zeit des Bauernkrieges, studiert ab 1506 an der Artistenfakultät, wechselt 1512 an die Universität in Frankfurt/Oder. Protestant theologian and social revolutionary during the Peasants' War, studied at the Faculty of Arts from 1506, transferred to the university in Frankfurt/Oder in 1512.

Ulrich von Hutten 1488–1523
Humanist, Publizist und Reichsritter, ab 1507 Philosophiestudium, gibt auch selbst Unterricht, erkrankt 1508 an Syphilis und verlässt überstürzt die Stadt. Humanist, writer and critic, Imperial Knight, from 1507 study of philosophy, taught as well, contracted syphilis in 1508 and rushed headlong out of town.

Georgius Agricola 1494–1555
Begründer der Montanwissenschaften und Chemnitzer Bürgermeister, von 1514 bis 1518 Studium der alten Sprachen, von 1522 bis 1523 Medizinstudium in Leipzig. Originator of mining science and Mayor of Chemnitz, in Leipzig study of classical languages from 1514 to 1518, and medicine from 1522 to 1523.

Joachim Camerarius 1500–1574
Humanist und Reformer, ab 1512 Ausbildung in Leipzig, von 1541 bis zum Tod Professor für Griechisch und Latein, dreimaliger Rektor, Freund von Melanchthon. Humanist and reformer, from 1512 education in Leipzig, from 1541 to his death, Professor of Greek and Latin, three times Rector, friend of Melanchthon.

Tycho Brahe 1546–1601
Astronom, ab 1562 Studium in Leipzig, hier erste astronomische Studien, verliert bei Duell wegen Streits um mathematische Formel einen Teil seiner Nase. Astronomer, from 1562 study and first astronomical studies in Leipzig, lost part of his nose in a duel following a quarrel over a mathematical formula.

Die Universität im 17. Jahrhundert The University in the 17th Century

PENNÄLER, LANGER KRIEG UND VORLESUNG IN DEUTSCHER SPRACHE
FRESHMEN, LONG WAR AND LECTURES IN THE GERMAN LANGUAGE

Gäbe es Anfang des 17. Jahrhunderts schon Boulevardzeitungen, dann würden Verbrechen an oder von Studenten die Schlagzeilen bestimmen: 14. Februar 1605 – Student beim Mummenlaufen erstochen ▪ 10. August 1608 – Student beim Sturm auf Haus eines Schneiders erstochen ▪ Fastnacht 1613 – Tumult zwischen Studenten und Schuhknechten ▪ 30. Januar 1615 – Studenten erstechen bei Tumult zwei Häscher ▪ 30. Mai 1626 – Student ersticht auf Dorf bei Leipzig einen Bauern beim Spiel ▪ 16. Dezember 1641 – Student verwundet Rechtskonsulent Grempler vor der Löwenapotheke …

Doch in der ersten Hälfte des Jahrhunderts existieren noch keine Tageszeitungen, vom Boulevard ganz zu schweigen. Also bleiben die Schlagzeilen aus. Dennoch zeigen die Daten, dass es um das Verhältnis zwischen den Bewohnern der Stadt Leipzig und den Studenten der Universität, die 1609 bereits 200 Jahre besteht, nach wie vor nicht zum Besten bestellt ist. Dass die Gewalt immer mehr zunimmt, ist typisch für dieses Jahrhundert. Wilhelm Bruchmüller schreibt in seinem Buch »Der Leipziger Student 1409 – 1909«: »Man begeht gewiß keinen Irrtum, wenn man das 17. Jahrhundert als die Zeit des tiefsten Tiefststandes studentischer Sittlichkeit überhaupt betrachtet.«

In manchen Darstellungen heißt es zudem, dass diese Sittenlosigkeit an evangelischen Universitäten stärker ausgeprägt sei als an katholischen. Schließlich hat sich das Studentenleben seit der Reformation gewaltig verändert. Die zuvor geltenden strengen Regeln sind außer Kraft gesetzt. Das Zusammenleben in den Bursen, wo die starke Reglementierung der Studier- und Lebensgemeinschaften durchgesetzt wurde, ist weitgehend zerfallen. Immer mehr Studenten wohnen jetzt in Alumnaten, also Wohnheimen, oder sogar zur Untermiete bei Bürgern der Stadt.

Had there been tabloids at the beginning of the 17th century, crimes against students and crimes committed by the students themselves would have dominated the headlines: 14 February 1605 – student stabbed while participating in *Mummenlaufen* (walking while wearing a mask) ▪ 10 August 1608 – student stabbed while raiding a tailor's house ▪ Shrove Tuesday 1613 – riots between students and cobblers ▪ 30 January 1615 – students stab two of their pursuers in a riot ▪ 30 May 1626 – student stabs a peasant while gambling in a village near Leipzig ▪ 16 December 1641 – student wounds legal advisor Grempler in front of *Löwenapotheke* (Lion's pharmacy)…

There were no daily newspapers in the first half of the 17th century though, let alone tabloids. Those headlines failed to appear. The data show, however, that the relationship between the citizens of Leipzig and the students of the University, which had existed for 200 years in 1609, was still not at its best. The ever growing violence was typical of this century. Wilhelm Bruchmüller wrote in his book, *Der Leipziger Student 1409 – 1909* ("The Leipzig Student 1409 – 1909"): "You certainly commit no error when you consider the 17th century as the time of the absolute lowest of the low in student morality."

Furthermore, some descriptions say that immorality was more prevalent at protestant universities than at catholic ones. Student life had enormously changed since the Reformation after all. The strict rules which had been in place so far were overturned. The shared existence in dorms, where the strictly regimented studying and living conditions within this community had been enforced, had largely collapsed. More and more students now lived in boarding schools, that is student residences, or even as subtenants with citizens of the city.

Von Leibniz entwickelte Rechenmaschine.
Calculating machine developed by Leibniz.

Gottfried Wilhelm Leibniz hat die Universität ein Denkmal gesetzt.
The University erected a monument to Gottfried Wilhelm Leibniz.

Titelseite der »Comoedia vom Studenten-Leben« von Johann Georg Schoch.
Front page of the "Comedy of Student Life" by Johann Georg Schoch.

NEUES PHÄNOMEN

Und noch etwas Neues entsteht zu Beginn des 17. Jahrhunderts: der Pennalismus. Zuerst an den Universitäten Leipzig und Jena beobachtet, breitet sich dieses Phänomen rasch aus. Haben die neuen Studenten das Ritual der Deposition hinter sich gebracht, beginnen für sie die Pennaljahre, die mindestens ein Jahr, sechs Monate und sechs Tage andauern. Die neu Immatrikulierten werden von älteren Semestern regelrecht dazu gezwungen, sich deren landsmannschaftlichen Organisationen anzuschließen. Dann müssen die Pennäler den höheren Semestern für Dienste zur Verfügung stehen, ihnen die Stube sauber halten, für frische Bekleidung sorgen, Botengänge erledigen. Beim Eintritt in die Pennaljahre haben sie einen »Acceßschmaus« zu bezahlen und nach Ablauf ihrer Zeit als Pennäler einen »Absolutionsschmaus«.

Nach und nach treiben es die älteren Jahrgänge immer wilder mit den Pennälern, etwa ab den 1640er-Jahren ist es Brauch, dass die jungen Studenten in möglichst abgerissener Kleidung herumlaufen, keinen Degen tragen und auch keinen langen Zopf, wie es sich für einen ordentlichen Studenten gehört. Vor allem die ärmeren Studiosi – und davon gibt es in Leipzig etliche – können sich mit den Umständen durchaus arrangieren, wie beispielsweise in der 1657 erschienenen »Comoedia vom Studenten-Leben« von Johann Georg Schoch in einigen Szenen beschrieben wird. Zudem bieten die eigenen Landsmannschaften auch Schutz nach außen.

Genau diese starke landsmannschaftliche Prägung und der aus ihr sprechende Nationalismus sowie die immer ungehemmteren Ausschreitungen der Studenten führen dazu, dass der Pennalismus von allen Seiten

NEW PHENOMENON

And another new phenomenon emerged at the beginning of the 17th century: *Pennalismus* (exploitation of first year students). This phenomenon, at first observed at the Universities of Leipzig and Jena, spread quickly. Once the new students had gone through the ritual of deposition, they began their years as freshmen, which would last for at least one year, six months and six days. The newly registered students were actually forced by the elder students to join their regional corporations. Then the freshmen had to be available to upper division students for services, and were required to keep their parlours clean, provide fresh clothes and run errands. When entering into their freshmen years, they had to pay for an "access feast" in addition to an "absolution feast" after having served their time.

By and by, the elder students overstepped their boundaries with the freshmen. From the 1640s, it became customary for the young students to walk around in clothes that were as ragged as possible. They neither wore a rapier nor a long braid which was considered suitable to a proper student. Mainly the poorer students – and there were many of them in Leipzig – could come to terms with those circumstances, as it was described, for instance, by Johann Georg Schoch in some scenes of the *Comoedia vom Studenten-Leben* ("Comedy of Student Life"), published in 1657. Furthermore, their own regional student corporations offered outward protection.

This strong compatriot identity and the nationalism stemming from it, as well as the ever more uninhibited actions of the students, resulted in the fight against *Pennalismus* from all sides. In their aim, the

Ab 1648 in Universitätsbesitz: Fürstenhaus mit Erker in der Grimmaischen Straße.
From 1648 in possession of the University: Fürstenhaus *with bay in* Grimmaische Straße.

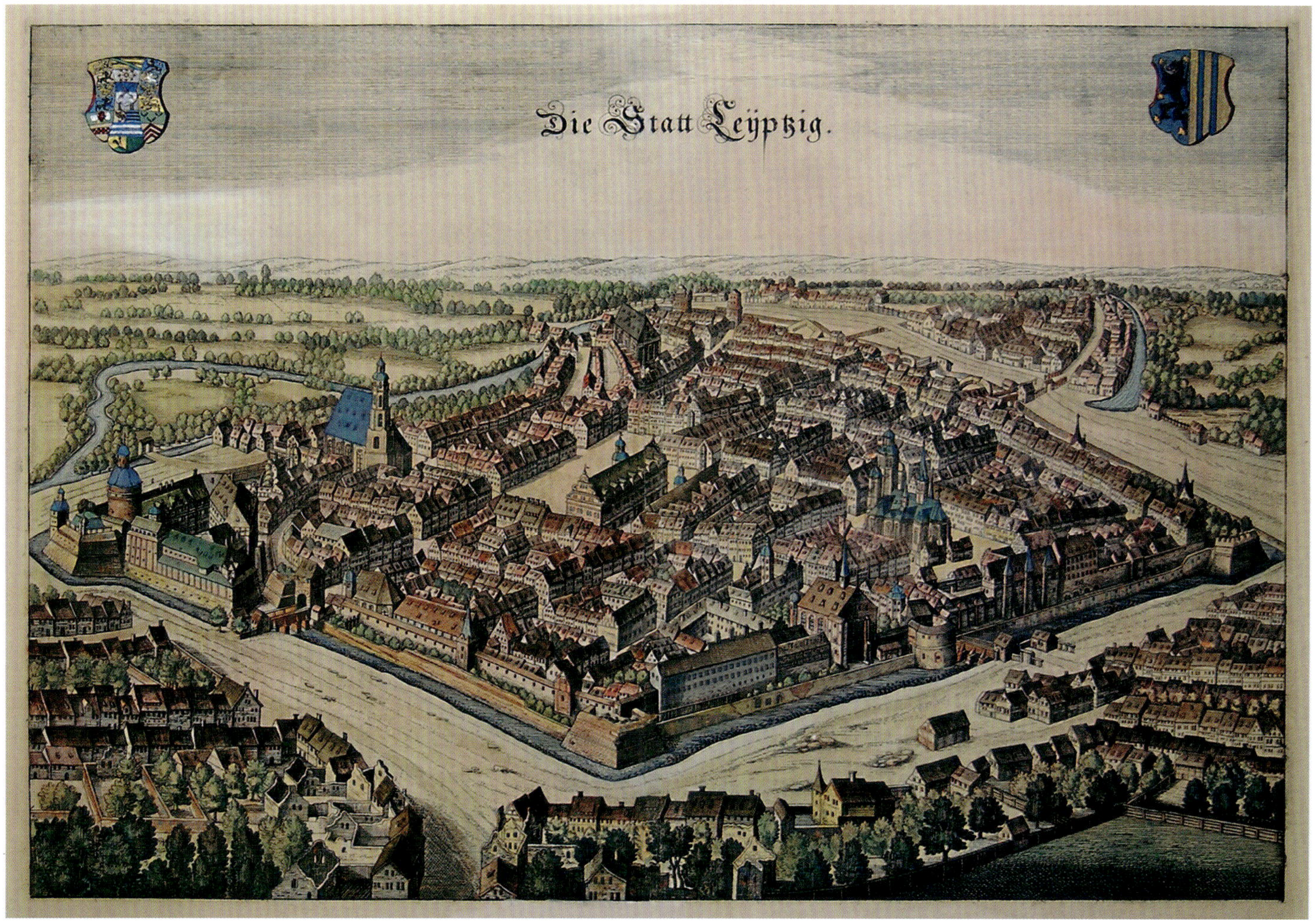

Leipziger Stadtansicht aus dem Jahr 1614.
View of the city of Leipzig from 1614.

bekämpft wird. Dabei ist die Obrigkeit – die Landesregierungen, die Universitäten und die Räte der Städte – zwar im Ziel einig, einen gemeinsamen Weg findet sie aber nicht. 1633 regt die Universität Wittenberg eine konzertierte Aktion gegen den Pennalismus an allen evangelischen deutschen Universitäten an. Leipzig lehnt mit der Begründung ab, Senat und Rektor hätten bereits große Erfolge vorzuweisen. 1657 einigen sich auf dem Reichstag zu Regensburg die dort vertretenen geistlichen und weltlichen Kurfürsten, die Reichsstädte, Grafen und Ritterorden auf ein Verbot. In Kursachsen wird dieses jedoch erst 1661 mit einem »Edikt und ernster Befehl zur gänzlichen Abschaffung des Pennalwesens auf der Universität von Leipzig« umgesetzt.

authorities – the provincial governments, the universities and the city councils – were united but they could not agree upon which path to take. In 1633, the University of Wittenberg initiated a concerted action against *Pennalismus* at all protestant German universities. Leipzig refused, stating that the Senate and Rector had already achieved great success. In 1657, electors of clergy and gentry, imperial cities, counts and orders of knights represented at the Diet of Regensburg agreed upon a ban. In the Electorate of Saxony, however, this ban was enforced as late as 1661, based on an "Edict and strict order for the complete abolition of *Pennalismus* at the University of Leipzig".

ZEITUNG UND FORSCHUNG

Eine Nachricht wie diese kann man in Leipzig nun tatsächlich schon in der Tageszeitung lesen. Vom 1. Juli 1650 an erscheint sechs Mal pro Woche ein politisches Nachrichtenblatt, herausgegeben von Timotheus Ritzsch, einem ortsansässigen Drucker. »Einkommende Zeitungen« heißt das zunächst vierseitige Blatt, da zu jener Zeit der Begriff Zeitung noch dem der Nachricht gleichgesetzt wird. Nicht nur das

NEWSPAPER AND RESEARCH

News items such as the one mentioned above could be read in a daily newspaper in Leipzig. A four-page political news bulletin, published by Timotheus Ritzsch, a local printer, was issued six times a week beginning 1 July 1650. It was called "Incoming Newspapers" as the term newspaper was equated with news in those days. The press itself had its origins in Leipzig, and the birthplace of research into the press

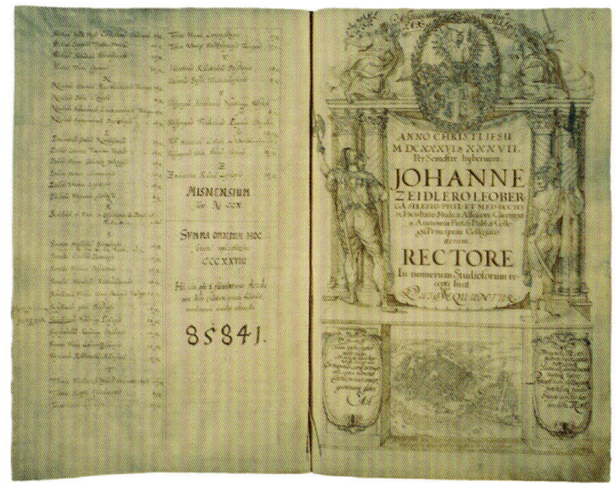

Matrikel-Schmuckblätter der Wintersemester 1635 und 1636 mit Motiven aus dem Dreißigjährigen Krieg.
Decorative pages of the winter semesters' 1635 and 1636 registers showing themes from the Thirty Years' War.

Zeitungswesen nimmt in Leipzig seinen Anfang, auch die Forschung zur Presse hat ihre Wiege an der Pleiße. Bereits in den 70er-Jahren des 17. Jahrhunderts setzt der Philosoph, Historiker und Theologe Otto Mencke in seinen Vorlesungen Zeitungsnachrichten ein. Er selbst gibt die erste deutsche Gelehrtenzeitschrift »Acta Eruditorium« heraus. Und 1690 wird in Leipzig auch die erste Dissertation zum Thema geschrieben. »De Relationibus Novellis« (»Über Zeitungsberichte«) lautet der Titel der Arbeit von Tobias Peucer, in der er sich mit der Entstehung und der Funktion der Presse beschäftigt. Was er herausarbeitet, lässt sich ohne weiteres auch auf heutige Presseerzeugnisse übertragen: Er sieht den Ursprung der Presse sowohl in der »menschlichen Neugierde« als

was at the *Pleiße* river as well. The philosopher, historian and theologian Otto Mencke used newspaper articles in his lectures as early as the 1670s. He published the first German academic journal "Acta Eruditorium" himself. The first dissertation on the topic was written in Leipzig in 1690. "De Relationibus Novellis" ("About Newspaper Reports") read the title of the work by Tobias Peucer, in which he addressed the formation and function of the press. His findings can be readily transferred to the current press: he saw that the origins of the press stemmed from both "human inquisitiveness" and the "quest for profit" by the people who amassed and sold news. The purpose of the paper was, according to Peucer, "the announcement of new events coupled with entertainment".

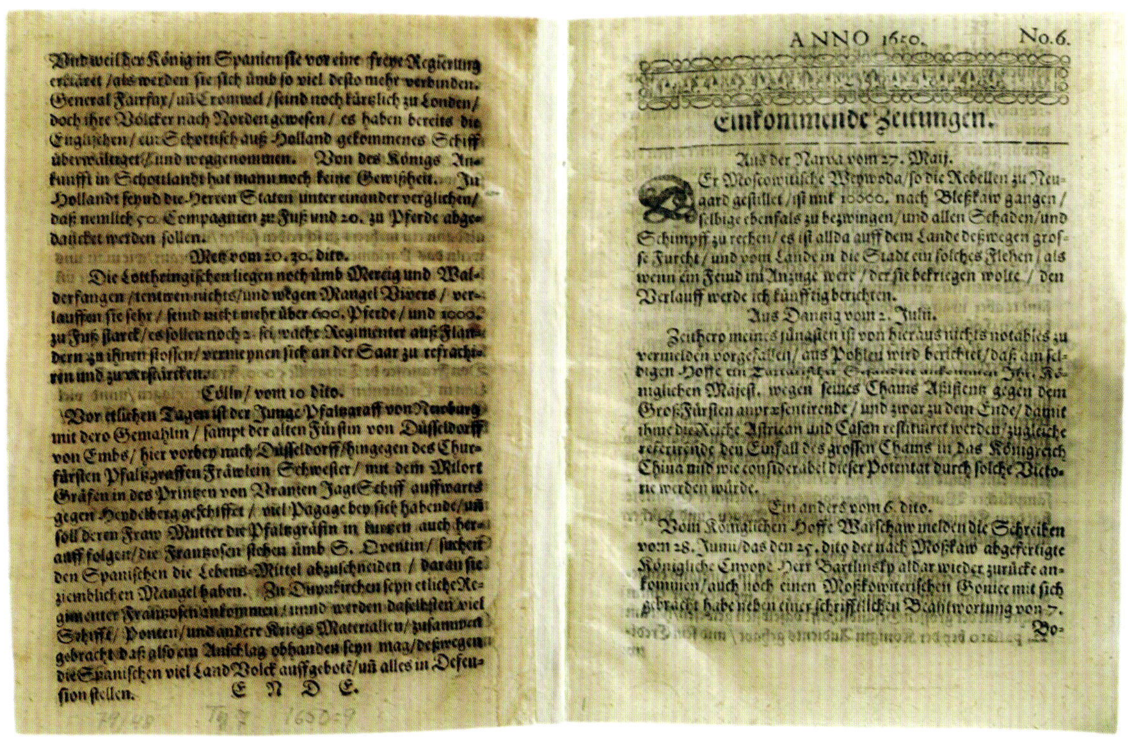
ANNO 1650. No.6.
Einkommende Zeitungen.
Aus der Narwa vom 27. Maij.
Aus Dantzig vom 2. Julii.
Ein anders vom 6. dito.
Meß vom 20. 30. dito.
Cölln / vom 10 dito.
E N D E.

Die erste Tageszeitung der Welt von Timotheus Ritzsch und das Signet der »Officin Ritschiana«.
The world's first daily newspaper by Timotheus Ritzsch and imprint of "Officin Ritschiana".

Links: Prunkvoller Grabstein in der Universitätskirche für den 1613 verstorbenen Studenten Johannes von Zesterfeldt.
Left: Pompous tombstone, in the University Church, of the student Johannes von Zesterfeldt, deceased in 1613.

Die Paulinerkirche, geistiges Zentrum der protestantischen Universität.
The Pauliner *Church, spiritual centre of the Protestant University.*

auch in der »Gewinnsucht« der Leute, die Neuigkeiten sammeln und verkaufen. Zweck der Zeitung ist Peucer zufolge die »Kenntnisgabe neuer Ereignisse, verbunden mit Unterhaltung«.

GEPLAGTE JURISTEN

Aber noch lange bevor diese Entwicklung einsetzt, sind Leipzig und Umgebung auch Schauplätze im Dreißigjährigen Krieg. Die Stadt wird mehrfach belagert und von Soldaten der verschiedenen Parteien überrannt, im September 1631 besiegen die vereinten Heere der Sachsen und Schweden in Breitenfeld das Aufgebot der Katholischen Liga. Ein gutes Jahr später treffen die verfeindeten Lager erneut bei Leipzig aufeinander, in Lützen kommt es zur entscheidenden Schlacht zwischen den Truppen Wallensteins und des Schwedenkönigs Gustav Adolf, der dabei den Tod findet.

Auch die Universität bleibt nicht vom Krieg verschont, wobei es die Juristenfakultät besonders hart trifft: Ihr in Richtung Pleißenburg gelegenes Gebäude wird zerstört. Die ihres Auditoriums beraubten

STRICKEN JURISTS

Long before this development began, Leipzig and its surroundings were scenes in the Thirty Years' War. The city was repeatedly besieged and overrun by soldiers of various parties. In September 1631, the united armies of the Saxons and Swedes defeated the contingent of the Catholic League in Breitenfeld. More than a year later the hostile parties encountered each other again near Leipzig, in Lützen. It culminated in the decisive battle between Wallenstein's troops and those of the Swedish King Gustav Adolf, who met his end there.

The University did not escape the war either, whereas the Faculty of Law was hit especially hard: its building facing the *Pleißenburg* castle was destroyed. The lecturers of law, deprived of their auditorium, had to beg for "scores of little rooms and parlours" at the other faculties. As if that were not enough, the town major seized the property and had – after the debris had been removed – soldiers' houses built on the premises. The jurists complained in 1657 about "all sorts of scoundrels" who had taken shelter in these buildings. These conditions were to last for more than 100 years as the property would not be returned until 1769. The Faculty was even billed 800 *Taler* for the derelict soldiers' houses.

REVIVAL OF THE CITY

The city was badly afflicted by the Thirty Years' War after all. The number of inhabitants decreased from 18,000 to 12,000 – which was not only due to the

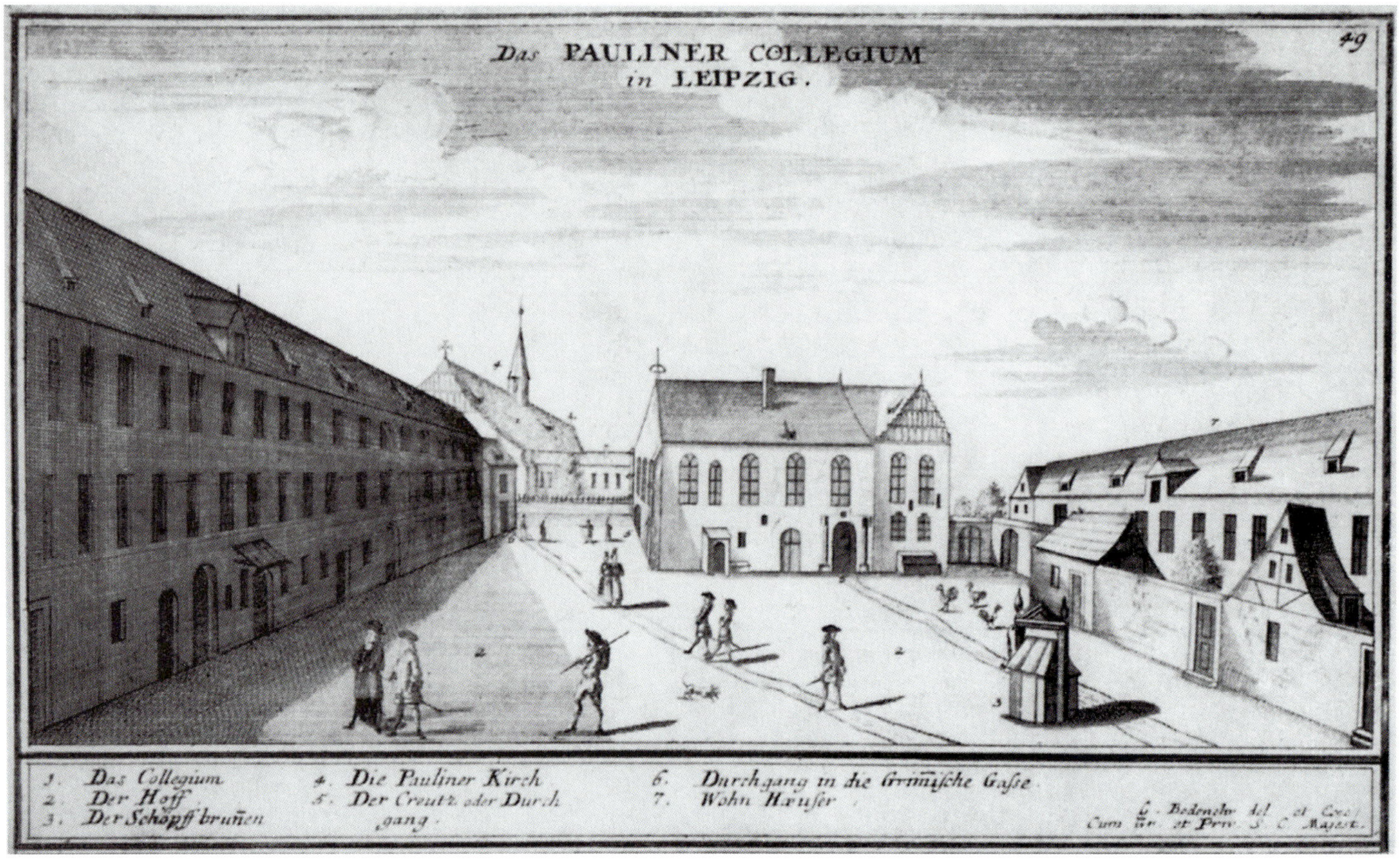

Mittelpaulinum am Ende des 17. Jahrhunderts.
Centre of Paulinum at the end of the 17th century.

Rechtslehrer müssen bei den anderen Fakultäten um »etliche Räumchen und Stuben« betteln. Als ob es damit nicht genug wäre, beschlagnahmt der Stadtkommandant den Grund und Boden und lässt – nachdem die Trümmer beseitigt sind – Soldatenhäuser auf dem Gelände bauen. 1657 beschweren sich die Juristen, dass in diesen Gebäuden »allerley Canaille« Unterschlupf gefunden habe. Mehr als 100 Jahre dauert dieser Zustand an. Erst 1769 werden Grund und Boden zurückgegeben, wobei der Fakultät für die heruntergekommenen Soldatenhäuser auch noch 800 Taler in Rechnung gestellt werden.

Wegbereiter der Aufklärung: Samuel von Pufendorf.
Precursor of enlightenment: Samuel von Pufendorf.

STÄDTISCHER AUFSCHWUNG

Insgesamt hat der Dreißigjährige Krieg der Stadt arg zugesetzt. Die Einwohnerzahl sinkt von 18 000 auf 12 000 Menschen, was nicht allein am Krieg liegt. So wütet etwa im Jahr 1637 die Pest, der mehr als 4 000 Menschen zum Opfer fallen. Trotz der Schäden durch Belagerung, Besetzung, plündernde und marodierende Soldaten erholt sich die Stadt erstaunlich schnell. Dank des Messeprivilegs und der sich immer stärker herausbildenden führenden Stellung als Buchhandelsplatz hat Leipzig bessere wirtschaftliche Voraussetzungen als andere deutsche Städte. Auch die Universität gelangt durch

war. The plague raged in 1637, claiming more than 4,000 lives. Leipzig recovered surprisingly fast despite the damages brought about by siege and occupation of the city, pillaging and marauding soldiers. Leipzig had better economic conditions than other German cities thanks to the trade fair privilege and its position evolved as a leading place of book trade. The University was revived through the interest of the Electors in extending and reconstructing the country: while the enrolments had only slowly increased during the 16th century, their number virtually exploded now. More than 1,100 people willing to learn registered per semester in peak periods. The University of Leipzig rose to become one of the most attended universities in Germany. Important scholars and students, who later would be noted in several fields of study, purposefully chose the University of Leipzig: the lyricist Paul Fleming studied there from 1628 to 1633; Samuel Pufendorf, who later became jurist and pioneer of enlightenment, enrolled at the University in 1645.

The city owed much to its citizens as well: advocate Huldreich Groß bequeathed his book collection comprising 4,000 volumes and all his assets to the Council of Leipzig in 1677, the only condition being that a library "to the benefit of the city's youth" be set up. This was realized in 1683. The Bibliotheca senatus Lipsiensis opened on the upper floor of the arsenal and cloth hall on the *Universitätsstraße*. Its stock continually grew through purchases and donations.

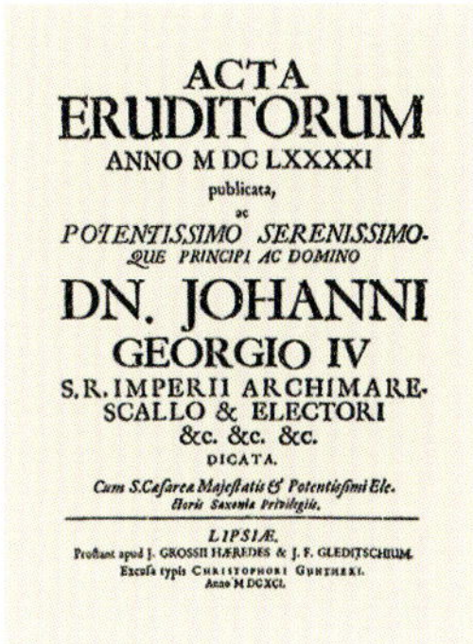

ACTA
ERUDITORUM
ANNO M DC LXXXXI
publicata,
ac
POTENTISSIMO SERENISSIMO-
QUE PRINCIPI AC DOMINO
DN. JOHANNI
GEORGIO IV
S.R.IMPERII ARCHIMARE-
SCALLO & ELECTORI
&c. &c. &c.
DICATA.
Cum S.Cæsareæ Majestatis & Potentissimi Ele-
ctoris Saxoniæ Privilegiis.

LIPSIÆ.
Prostant apud J. GROSSII HÆREDES & J. F. GLEDITSCHIUM.
Excusa typis CHRISTOPHORI GUNTHERI.
Anno M DCXCI.

Links: Otto Mencke und die von ihm herausgegebene »Acta Eruditorum«.
Left: Otto Mencke and the "Acta Eruditorum" published by him.

Bursa Bavarica am Nikolaikirchhof.
Bursa Bavarica at St. Nicholas churchyard.

das Interesse der Kurfürsten am Landesausbau und Wiederaufbau zu neuer Blüte: War die Zahl der Immatrikulationen im Laufe des 16. Jahrhunderts nur langsam gestiegen, so explodieren nun die Zahlen geradezu. In Spitzenzeiten melden sich bis zu 1 100 Lernwillige pro Semester an. Die Leipziger Universität steigt zu einer der meistbesuchten in Deutschland auf. Bedeutende Gelehrte und Studenten, die später in verschiedenen Fachrichtungen von sich reden machen sollten, wählen die Universität Leipzig gezielt aus: So studiert hier von 1628 bis 1633 der Lyriker Paul Fleming, 1645 schreibt sich der spätere Rechtsgelehrte und Wegbereiter der Aufklärung Samuel Pufendorf in die Matrikel ein.

Auch ihren Bürgern verdankt die Stadt viel: Advokat Huldreich Groß vermacht im Jahr 1677 dem Leipziger Rat seine rund 4 000 Bände umfassende Büchersammlung und zudem sein gesamtes Vermögen. Einzige Auflage: In Leipzig soll eine Bibliothek »zum Nutzen der studierenden Stadtjugend« entstehen. Verwirklicht wird dies 1683. In einem Saal im ersten Obergeschoss des Zeug- und Gewandhauses an der Universitätsstraße öffnet die Bibliotheca senatus Lipsiensis. Durch Käufe und Schenkungen wächst ihr Bestand stetig.

Zwischen 1678 und 1687 wird im Stil des italienischen und niederländischen Barocks am Naschmarkt die

The *Handelsbörse* (trade stock exchange) was built in Italian and Dutch baroque style in the *Naschmarkt* square between 1678 and 1687, initiated by 30 large-scale merchants. It served as a place of assembly and commerce for about 200 years. Some years later, the student Lessing was very fond of the city representing "the whole world in microcosm" and his fellow student Goethe considered the modern Leipzig a welcomed contrast to the "cramped conditions" of his hometown of Frankfurt, even though the buildings of the University were far from shining in new splendour. Several parts of the premises belonging to the former monastery remained

Engel von einem Epitaph aus dem Jahr 1685 in der Paulinerkirche.
Angel from an epitaph from the year 1685 in Pauliner *Church.*

Leipziger Stadtsiegel.
Leipzig Town Seal.

Handelsbörse erbaut – auf Initiative von 30 Großkaufleuten. Rund 200 Jahre lang dient sie als Versammlungsort und Handelsplatz. Der Student Lessing ist einige Jahre später sehr angetan von der »ganzen Welt im Kleinen«, und sein Kommilitone Goethe sieht das moderne Leipzig als willkommenen Kontrast zur »quetschenden Enge« seiner Vaterstadt Frankfurt, auch wenn die Gebäude der Universität alles andere als in neuem Glanz erstrahlen. Mehrere Teile des alten Klosterareals bleiben baufällig, was Poesieprofessor Joachim Feller zu einem Vergleich mit den vor Mist strotzenden Ställen des sagenhaften Königs Augias veranlasst: »Das Leipziger Paulinum erscheint ungeordnet und verschmutzt … (wie) ein neuer Augiasstall.«

DYNASTIEN UND DUELLE

Aufschwung und Erneuerung spiegeln sich in den Fachdisziplinen zunächst nicht wider. Die Universität gilt nach wie vor als eine der wissenschaftlich konservativsten Hochschulen in Deutschland. Geprägt ist sie unter anderem durch wahre Gelehrtendynastien, die an den Lehrstühlen der Theologischen und der Juristischen Fakultät den Ton angeben. Es dauert noch lange, bis sich die konservative Grundausrichtung ändert, bis die junge kritische Intelligenz sich gegen die veralteten Auffassungen, die lutherisch-orthodoxen Lehrinhalte und die dogmatische Lehrweise auflehnt. Sympathisanten und Förderer der frühen Aufklärung

dilapidated, which prompted professor of poetry Joachim Feller to compare them to the stables of the legendary King Augeas which were bursting with filth: "The Leipzig Paulinum appears disorderly and filthy… (as) a new Augean stable."

DYNASTIES AND DUELS

Revival and renewal did not reflect in the special disciplines at first. The University was still considered one of the most scholarly conservative institutions of higher learning in Germany. It was shaped, among others, by true scholarly dynasties that set the tone at the chairs of the Faculties of Theology and Law. It took a long time until this fundamental conservative orientation would change, until the young and critical intelligentsia took a stand against the outmoded concepts, the Lutheran-Orthodox course content and the dogmatic teaching methods. Sympathizers and proponents of the early enlightenment are by all means to be found at the Alma mater Lipsiensis at the end of the 17th century, such as the jurist Christian Thomasius. In 1687 he caused a great stir when he announced a lecture would be held in the German language. This made him the first to directly attack the predominance of Latin as the binding and international scholarly language up to that time.

Authorities and the University's institutions had yet to deal with a very different phenomenon: There were a growing number of known cases of students taking part in duels. Bloody one-on-one battles were nothing new indeed, but until the middle of the 17th century

Die 1679 eingeweihte Handelsbörse am Naschmarkt.
The Handelsbörse, *inaugurated in 1679 at the* Naschmarkt *square.*

sind zum Ende des 17. Jahrhunderts an der Alma mater Lipsiensis durchaus zu finden. So erregt der Jurist Christian Thomasius 1687 großes Aufsehen, als er eine in deutscher Sprache gehaltene Vorlesung ankündigt. Damit ist er der erste, der die Alleinherrschaft des Latein als bis dahin verbindlich geltende, internationale Gelehrtensprache ganz direkt angreift.

Noch aber haben die Behörden und die universitären Institutionen sich mit einem ganz anderen Phänomen herumzuschlagen: Zunehmend werden Fälle bekannt, in denen Studenten sich an Duellen beteiligen. Zwar sind blutige Zweikämpfe nichts Neues, aber bis Mitte des 17. Jahrhunderts sind es eher Schlägereien, die keinen Regeln folgen und ausgetragen werden, wenn sich ein Student in seiner Ehre gekränkt fühlt.

Die Behörden wollen der Entwicklung mit allen Mitteln entgegenwirken. Am 26. November 1665 wird ein rigoroses Duellverbot erlassen, das aber keine Wirkung zeigt und am 8. November 1670 durch ein erneutes scharfes, so genanntes Duellmandat wiederholt wird. Dennoch sterben weiter Menschen im Zweikampf, so am 15. Februar 1677 der Student Baron von Maydel, der von Offizieren der Leipziger Garnison getötet wird. Die Duelle haben inzwischen eine neue Dimension angenommen: Neben Stichwaffen wie Degen oder Rapieren kommen zunehmend Feuerwaffen zum Einsatz.

VERKANNTE GENIES

In den letzten Jahren des 17. Jahrhunderts werden noch einige Weichen gestellt: 1690 lehnt sich Christian Thomasius, einer der Väter der deutschen Aufklärung, zunächst gegen die Lehre der gottgewollten Obrigkeit auf. Die von ihm herausgegebenen »Monatshefte« gelten als erste deutschsprachige wissenschaftliche Zeitschrift. Als er dann auch noch gegen die offizielle Politik des Dresdner Hofs in einer fürstlichen Eheangelegenheit Stellung bezieht, wird ein Lehr-, Disputations- und Veröffentlichungsverbot gegen ihn erlassen, worauf er Leipzig den Rücken kehrt und in Halle an der Saale eine neue Universität aufbaut.

Auch der letzte Universalgelehrte Gottfried Wilhelm Leibniz verlässt die Leipziger Universität in Richtung Nürnberg. Er wird verkannt von den Professoren, die sein Promotionsgesuch ablehnen. Als 20-Jähriger ist er ihnen schlichtweg zu jung, dabei wurde er schon im Alter von 15 Jahren immatrikuliert. Zwei Jahrhunderte später wird ihm die Universität ein Denkmal setzen.

Blick auf das Collegium Paulinum.
View of the Collegium Paulinum.

these were rather brawls that did not follow any rules and erupted when a student felt dishonoured.

Authorities wanted to counteract this development by all means. On 26 November 1665, a rigorous ban on duels was enacted, which made no impact, and was replaced by a renewed restriction, the so-called *Duellmandat* on 8 November 1670. Nevertheless people continued to die in one-to-one battles: on 15 February 1677, the student Baron von Maydel, was killed by officers from the Leipzig garrison. Duels had taken on a new dimension by that time. Besides thrusting weapons such as the epee and the rapier, firearms were increasingly used.

Fechtende Studenten mit Rapier und Dolch.
Fencing students with rapier and dagger.

UNDERESTIMATED GENIUSES

Some other agents of change set the course during the last years of the 17th century: in 1690 Christian Thomasius, one of the fathers of German enlightenment, at first, opposed the teachings pertaining to divine law. The "Monthly Magazines" published by Thomasius were considered the first German scholarly journals. When he later took a stand against the public politics of the Dresden court in a sovereign's marriage issue, a teaching, dispute and publishing ban was enacted against him. Thereupon he turned his back on Leipzig and set up a new university in Halle on the river Saale.

Also, the last polymath, Gottfried Wilhelm Leibniz, left the University of Leipzig and headed towards Nuremberg. He was underestimated by the professors who refused his application for a doctorate. As a 20-year-old, they considered him utterly too young, although he had been enrolled at the age of 15. The University would erect a monument to him two centuries later.

Orgel aus der ersten Hälfte des 17. Jahrhunderts in der Musikinstrumenten-Sammlung der Universität.
Organ from the first half of the 17th century in the collection of musical instruments at the University.

Schmuckblatt der Matrikel 1601 mit Schwur auf Jesus Christus und Universitätszeptern.

Decorative page of the students' register of 1601 with oath to Jesus Christ and University sceptres.

Matrikel vom Sommersemester 1639 mit Bildnis des neuen Rektors Andreas Rivinus.

Students' register from the summer semester of 1639, with portrait of the new Rector Andreas Rivinus.

DAS 17. JAHRHUNDERT
THE 17TH CENTURY

BLICK IN DIE WELT
VIEW OF THE WORLD

1618 Böhmische Protestanten lösen mit dem Prager Fenstersturz den Dreißigjährigen Krieg aus. Bohemian Protestants trigger the Thirty Years' War with the Defenestration of Prague.

1626 Holländer kaufen die Halbinsel Manhattan und errichten Neu-Amsterdam. Dutchmen buy the peninsula Manhattan and establish New Amsterdam.

1632 Rembrandt van Rijn malt sein berühmtes Werk »Die Anatomie des Dr. Tulp«. Rembrandt van Rijn paints his famous work "The Anatomy Lesson of Dr. Nicolaes Tulp".

1633 Das Inquisitionsgericht in Rom verurteilt Galileo Galilei zu lebenslangem Arrest. The Court of the Inquisition in Rome condemns Galileo Galilei to life imprisonment.

1642 Der mongolische Fürst Gushri Khan erklärt den Dalai Lama zur obersten Autorität in Tibet. Mongolian Prince Gushri Khan declares the Dalai Lama to be the ultimate authority in Tibet.

1643 Ludwig XIV. wird im Alter von vier Jahren zum französischen König gekrönt. Louis XIV is crowned King of France at the age of four.

1666 Molière bringt »Der Menschenfeind« auf die Bühne. Molière stages "Le Misanthrope".

1672 Isaac Newton stellt der Royal Society in London das erste Spiegelteleskop vor. Isaac Newton demonstrates the first reflecting telescope to the Royal Society in London.

1675 Preußen besiegt Schweden und Frankreich in der Schlacht bei Fehrbellin. Prussia defeats Sweden and France in the Battle of Fehrbellin.

1679 Englands Parlament schafft mit der Habeas-Corpus-Akte rechtsstaatliche Sicherheiten. Parliament of England establishes constitutional security by the Habeas Corpus Act.

1681 Der französische Physiker Denis Papin lässt sich seinen Schnellkochtopf patentieren. The French physicist Denis Papin has his pressure cooker patented.

1696 Zar Peter der Große tritt die Alleinherrschaft in Russland an. Tsar Peter the Great establishes his autocratic rule over Russia.

1697 Spanische Eroberer vernichten den letzten Staat der Maya in Mittelamerika. Spanish conquerors wipe out the last state of the Maya in Central America.

BERÜHMTHEITEN AN DER UNIVERSITÄT
ILLUSTRIOUS PEOPLE AT THE UNIVERSITY

Benedict Carpzov d. J. 1595–1666
Strafrechtler, Hexentheoretiker und Rechtswissenschaftler, ab 1648 Ordinarius der Juristischen Fakultät und Vorsitzender des Leipziger Schöppenstuhls. Criminal law expert, witch theorist and jurist, from 1648 professor at the Faculty of Law and chairman of the Leipzig board of layman accessors.

Otto von Guericke 1602–1686
Begründer der Vakuumtechnik, Erfinder der Kolbenluftpumpe, Magdeburger Bürgermeister, 1617 bis 1619 Studium an der Leipziger Artistenfakultät. Founder of the vacuum technology, inventor of the piston vacuum pump, Mayor of Magdeburg, study at the Faculty of Arts in Leipzig from 1617 to 1619.

Paul Fleming 1609–1640
Arzt und Schrifsteller, bedeutender Lyriker des Barock, nach Besuch der Leipziger Thomasschule von 1628 bis 1633 Studium der Medizin an der Universität. Physician and writer, important lyricist of the Baroque, after completion of Leipzig Thomas school study of medicine at the University from 1628 to 1633.

Christian Thomasius 1655–1728
Leipziger Jurist, Philosoph und Hochschulreformer, hält 1687 die erste Vorlesung in deutscher Sprache, kämpft erfolgreich gegen die Hexenprozesse. Leipzig jurist, philosopher and reformer of academia, delivered the first ever lecture in German in 1687, successfully fought against the witchcraft trials.

Gottfried Welsch 1618–1690
Begründer der Rechtsmedizin, Leipziger Stadtphysikus, Medizinprofessor, ab 1665 Rektor der Universität, ab 1668 Dekan der Medizinischen Fakultät. Founder of forensic medicine, Leipzig city physician, professor of medicine, from 1665 Rector of the University, from 1668 Dean of the Faculty of Medicine.

REICHE STADT, ARME STUDENTEN UND VIELE PROMINENTE

RICH CITY, POOR STUDENTS AND MANY NOTABLES

Zu Beginn des 18. Jahrhunderts lässt Leipzig als Buchstadt Frankfurt am Main deutlich hinter sich: Während in der Hessenmetropole im Jahr 1700 gerade einmal 88 Titel erscheinen, sind es an der Pleiße 276. Die Verlage haben sich zu großen Arbeitgebern entwickelt. So beschäftigt der Erfinder des Notentypendrucks, Johann Gottlob Immanuel Breitkopf, allein mehr als 100 Mitarbeiter. Bis zur Jahrhundertwende steigt die Buchproduktion auf jährlich 1 600 Titel.

Doch nicht nur der Buchdruck und die Verlage prägen das Gesicht der Stadt, auch andere Gewerbe breiten sich aus. So existieren Mitte des 18. Jahrhunderts elf Seiden- und Samtmanufakturen, sieben Silber- und Goldspinnereien, zahlreiche Woll- und auch Baumwollverarbeiter, Rauch- und Schnupftabakshäuser, Hersteller von Blasinstrumenten, Tapeten und Buntpapier. Da in den Stadtgrenzen noch einige Zeit lang Zunftschranken herrschen, siedeln sich viele Manufakturen im Umland an. In der Stadt dagegen erblüht das Handwerk. 1784 werden 296 Schneider-, 186 Schuhmacher-, 63 Kürschner- und 47 Strumpfwirkermeister gezählt, nicht zu vergessen die 104 Perücken- und 30 Knopfmacher – es zeigt sich, dass die Leipziger Bürger der luxuriösen Mode durchaus geneigt sind. Der Schriftsteller Jean Paul, der von 1781 bis 1784 in Leipzig studiert, merkt deshalb an: »Die Mode ist der Tyrann, der diese Stadt beherrscht.«

At the beginning of the 18th century, Leipzig clearly outpaced Frankfurt am Main as a city of books: in 1700 a mere 88 titles were published in the Hessian metropolis and 276 were issued at the *Pleiße* river. Publishing houses had developed into the largest employers in Leipzig. The inventor of musical score printing with movable type, Johann Gottlob Immanuel Breitkopf alone had a staff of more than 100. Book production grew to 1,600 titles yearly until the turn of the century.

However, not only printing and publishing shaped the townscape, other trades expanded as well. Around the middle of the 18th century, there were eleven silk and velvet manufacturers, seven silver and gold spinning mills, wool and cotton processing companies, tobacco and snuff companies, manufacturers of wind instruments, of wallpaper and coloured paper. As guild boundaries would be in existence within the city limits for some time, many manufacturers settled in the surrounding areas. Trade, however, flourished in the city. In 1784, Leipzig numbered 296 master taylors amongst its population, as well as 186 master cobblers, 63 master furriers and 47 master stocking knitters, not to mention the 104 wigmakers and 30 button makers – the Leipzig citizens proved to be definitely inclined to luxurious fashion. The writer Jean Paul, who studied in Leipzig from 1781 to 1784, remarked: "Fashion is the tyrant that rules this town."

Pokal aus dem Schatz der Polnischen Nation.
Goblet from the treasure of the Polish nation.

»Literaturpapst« und Rektor Johann Christoph Gottsched.
"Leading literary pundit" and Rector Johann Christoph Gottsched.

REVOLUTIONÄRE VERÄNDERUNGEN

An der Universität machen die frühen Aufklärer von sich reden, doch es gibt noch immer etliche Professoren, die der althergebrachten akademischen Ordnung huldigen. Aus dem Jahr 1742 ist die Klage von Studenten bekannt, die sich beschweren, dass trotz der Faulheit von Lehrkräften »unseren Eltern so viel Seufzer, Tränen und Geld ausgepreßt« werden. Sie führen einen gewissen Boerner an, der nach ihren Worten das ruhige Leben überaus zu schätzen weiß. »Er nimmt des Jahres über 2 500 Taler ein, besitzt alle Beneficia in der Stadt und auf dem Lande, wird reich und groß, läßt sich anbeten, arbeitet aber niemals den Wert eines Hellers dafür. Er steht früh um neun Uhr auf, setzt sich zu seiner Frau hin und nimmt ein Schälchen Kaffee und die Tabakspfeife in die Hand, verläßt die Frau nicht eine Stunde, und dieses währt, bis er zu Tisch geht. Nach Tisch legt er sich um zwei Uhr nieder und schläft bis halb fünf. Hernach trinkt er wieder Kaffee oder Schokolade und raucht Tabak bis in die Nacht. Alsdann geht man wieder zu Bett, und dieses treibt man jahraus, jahrein.«

Dennoch ist das 18. Jahrhundert von revolutionären Veränderungen in der Leipziger Wissenschaft geprägt: Aus der Medizin gehen die Chemie und die Botanik als neue Fachrichtungen hervor. Ökonomie und Technik halten Einzug an der Universität, es gibt erste Experimente mit der Elektrizität. Erich Brandenburg allerdings schreibt in einem Aufsatz nicht unbedingt Rühmliches über die Universität: »Ruhig, arbeitsam

REVOLUTIONARY CHANGES

The early proponents of enlightenment made a name for themselves at the University, but there were still numerous professors who rendered homage to the long-established academic structure. Students had been known to complain in 1742, that, despite the laziness of the teaching staff, "so many sighs and tears, and so much money are squeezed out of our parents." They mentioned a certain Mr. Boerner who, in their words, was known to have appreciated a relaxed way of life: "He draws more than 2,500 *Taler* per year, owns all beneficia in the city and in the countryside, becomes rich and a bigwig, has people worship him, but never works a Heller's worth for it. He gets up at nine o'clock in the morning, sits with his wife and takes a small bowl of coffee and his pipe in his hands; he does not leave his wife for a second, and this lasts until he sits down at table. After eating he lies down at two o'clock and sleeps until half past four. Thereafter he drinks coffee again or chocolate and smokes tobacco far into the night. Thereupon he goes to bed again, and carries on in this manner year in, year out."

The 18th century, nevertheless, was shaped by revolutionary changes in the area of science in Leipzig: chemistry and botany emerged as new fields of science originating from medicine. Economics and engineering found their way into the University, and there were the first experiments with electricity. Erich Brandenburg, nevertheless, wrote in his essay some unflattering comments about the University: "Laid-back,

Die »Große Feuerkugel« am Neumarkt mit Goethes Studentenwohnung.
The "Great Fireball" at the Neumarkt *with Goethe's student dwelling.*

Blick auf Leipzig um 1790 aus westlicher Richtung.
View of Leipzig from the west around 1790.

und gedankenarm floß in Leipzig auch in der zweiten Hälfte des 18. Jahrhunderts das akademische Leben dahin; nur in einzelnen Fachwissenschaften wurde Namhaftes geleistet, wie in der Philosophie durch Ernesti.«

Ob es an der Alma mater Lipsiensis im 18. Jahrhundert tatsächlich zumindest arbeitsam zugeht, darf bezweifelt werden. In »Leipzig im Profil. Ein Taschenwörterbuch für Einheimische und Fremde« heißt es nämlich: »Im ganzen findet man unter den hiesigen Studenten nicht den Fleiß, den man in Halle, Jena und Göttingen sieht, doch dürften sie leicht fleißiger sein als die Wittenberger. Das preußische Landeskind, das in Halle Theologie studiert, geht mit zwei Jahren von der Universität und nimmt dann so viel Wissenschaft, wenigstens theologische, mit nach Hause als der, der bei uns viertehalb und vier Jahre studiert hat.«

Allen Unkenrufen zum Trotz: Die Universität steht während der Aufklärung im Mittelpunkt deutscher und europäischer Wissenschaft und zieht damit auch viele Prominente an. So wird 1730 Johann Christoph Gottsched zum Professor für Poesie und Rhetorik berufen. Um ihn und seine Ehefrau scharen sich alsbald zahlreiche Literaten. Diese wiederum sorgen dafür, dass aus dem von früher bekannten Jahrmarktsspiel ein ernst zu nehmendes deutsches Nationaltheater entsteht, das die Ideale des Bürgertums transportiert. Eine weitere herausragende Persönlichkeit an der Universität ist Christian Fürchtegott Gellert, der 1734 als Student nach Leipzig kommt und von 1751 an Philosophie lehrt. Durch ihn und Gottsched entwickelt sich die Stadt zu einem literarischen Zentrum.

Gottscheds Wohnhaus »Goldener Bär« am Alten Neumarkt.
Gottsched's domicile "Golden Bear" at the old Neumarkt.

Und selbst wenn Frauen an der Universität noch nicht geduldet sind, ist es eine Frau, die im Umfeld Gottscheds für eine Revolution des Theaters sorgt: Friederike Caroline Neuber. 1727 gründet sie eine eigene Theatertruppe, nur zehn Jahre später vertreibt sie in einer symbolischen Handlung die Figur des Hanswurst von der Bühne. Selbst als Charakterdarstellerin gelobt, führt die Neuberin das Rollenstudium ein und sorgt damit für die originalgetreue Wiedergabe von Schauspieltexten.

hard-working and lacking in mental agility, this is how academic life floated about in Leipzig in the second half of the 18th century. Considerable results were achieved by only some individuals within certain branches of science, such as philosophy, by Ernesti."

It is doubtful that the people were really hard-working at the Alma mater Lipsiensis in the 18th century. The book *Leipzig im Profil. Ein Taschenwörterbuch für Einheimische und Fremde* ("Leipzig profile. A pocket dictionary for natives and foreigners") read: "On the whole, among local students, one cannot find the diligence to be seen in Halle, Jena and Göttingen, but they might be more diligent than those in Wittenberg. The Prussian subject, who studies theology in Halle, leaves university after two years and absorbs as much science, at least theological, as one who has studied here three and a half or four years."

Despite all prophecies of doom: during the period of enlightenment the University took centre stage in German and European science and hence attracted many notables as well, such as Christoph Gottsched, who was appointed professor of poetry and rhetoric in 1730. It was not long before numerous literati gathered around him and his wife. They enabled the development of a more serious German national theatre, which evolved from the earlier funfair plays. This new national theatre proliferated the ideals of the bourgeoisie among the population. Christian Fürchtegott Gellert, who came to Leipzig as a student in 1734 and taught philosophy from 1751, was another outstanding personality at the University. Through him and Gottsched the city developed into a centre of literature.

Even though women are not yet tolerated at the University, it was a woman from Gottsched's background, who revolutionized the theatre: Friederike Caroline Neuber. She founded her own theatre group in 1727. Only ten years later, she drove the character of Harlequin from the stage in a symbolic act. Having been praised as character actress herself, the *Neuberin* introduced role study and hence saw to the rendering of drama texts true to the original.

Der junge Student Goethe als Denkmal auf dem Leipziger Naschmarkt.
Monument of the young student Goethe in the Leipzig Naschmarkt.

HOCHDOTIERTE PROFESSOREN

Die Wirtschaft in Leipzig wächst – und mit ihr auch das Einkommen mancher Schichten. Während eine Wäscherin oder Magd mit 50 Talern im Jahr auskommen muss, können Maurer- oder Zimmergesellen immerhin schon 100 Taler für sich verbuchen. Ein hochdotierter Universitätsprofessor bringt es dagegen auf mehr als 2 500 Taler und hat damit mehr Geld zum Leben als ein Bürgermeister mit rund 1 800 Talern. Dagegen nimmt sich das Gehalt eines gewissen Johann Sebastian Bach, ab 1723 Thomaskantor, bescheiden aus: 100 Taler und 15 Groschen stehen auf seinem Gehaltszettel, wobei der Kantor Nebeneinnahmen von 600 Talern im Jahr durch so genannte Leichengelder und Brautmessen erzielen kann. Auch für Auftragskompositionen lässt sich Bach gut bezahlen: So erhält er 50 Taler für eine Huldigungskantate auf das sächsische Königspaar und die bevorstehende Vermählung der Prinzessin Maria Amalia mit Karl IV. von Sizilien. Auftraggeber nicht nur dieses Werkes ist die Universität.

In der Stadt zeigt sich der Reichtum der Bürger nicht allein in den Gebäuden. 1701 geht die Straßenbeleuchtung in Betrieb: 700 Rüböl-Laternen spenden Licht. Da die Stadt sich vor randalierenden Studenten fürchtet, wird diesen zugleich verboten, nachts mit Schlafröcken, Nachtmützen und brennenden Pfeifen durch die Straßen zu ziehen. Genützt hat es offenbar nicht viel, noch 1713 kommt es um der Schlafrockfreiheit willen zu Aufruhr, viele Studenten werden verhaftet.

HIGHLY REMUNERATED PROFESSORS

The economy in Leipzig grew – and with it the income of many a social class. While a laundress or maidservant had to make ends meet on 50 *Taler* a year, journeymen bricklayers or carpenters could take in 100 *Taler*. A highly remunerated university professor, however, managed to earn more than 2,500 *Taler* and hence had more money to live on than a mayor, who on the contrary, drew a salary of approximately 1,800 *Taler*. The salary of a certain Johann Sebastian Bach, Cantor at St. Thomas Church from 1723, appeared modest by comparison: 100 *Taler* and 15 *Groschen* were recorded on his pay slip. The Cantor could, on the other hand, achieve an additional income of 600 *Taler* a year by so-called corpse money or bridal masses. Bach got paid handsomely for compositions on commission: he received 50 *Taler* for a homage cantata to the Saxon royal couple and the imminent marriage of Princess Maria Amalia to Charles IV of Sicily. The University was the ordering party of this and other works.

In the city, the prosperity of the citizens not only showed in the surrounding buildings, but in the street lighting as well: 700 rapeseed oil lamps, which were implemented in 1701, dispensed light. As the city feared rioting students, the latter were forbidden to prowl the streets wearing nightgowns, nightcaps and burning pipes. Obviously this was to no avail. In 1713, riots occurred for the freedom to wear nightgowns in the streets and many students were arrested.

UNTERSCHIEDLICHER BROTERWERB

Dem bürgerlichen Reichtum stehen nicht nur die in ärmlichen Verhältnissen lebenden Handwerker gegenüber, sondern auch zahlreiche arme Studenten, sodass bisweilen von der »universitas pauperum«, der Hochschule der Armen, gesprochen wird. Statistisch betrachtet stellt die Theologische Fakultät die meisten armen Studenten, während deren Zahl bei den Juristen am geringsten ist. »Jeder Tagelöhner läßt seinen Sohn studieren, sobald er ihn nur auf der Schule vor dem Verhungern sichern kann; wovon er einst auf der Universität leben soll, daran wird nicht gedacht«, kritisiert Anselmus Rabiosus der Jüngere – mit richtigem Namen Andreas Georg Friedrich Rebmann – in seinen »Wanderungen und Kreuzzügen durch einen Teil Deutschlands«.

Rechts: Quittung Johann Sebastian Bachs für die Universität über die Zahlung von 58 Talern.
Right: Receipt from Johann Sebastian Bach to the University, certifying the payment of 58 Taler.

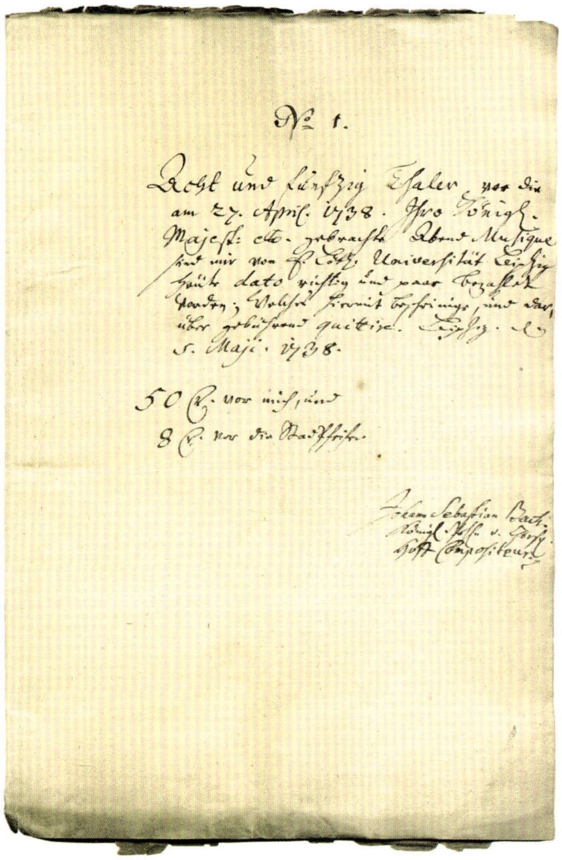

No 1.

Acht und funfzig Thaler, vor die am 27. April 1738. Ihro Königl. Majest. etc. gebrachte Abend Musique sind mir von E. Löbl. Universität Leipzig heute dato richtig und baar bezahlet worden, welche hiermit bescheinige, und darüber gebührend quittire. Leipzig d. 5. Maji 1738.

50 Th. vor mich, und
8 Th. vor die Stadtpfeifer.

Johann Sebastian Bach
Königl. Pohl. u. Churf.
Hoff Compositeur

Hörsaal der Juristenfakultät im 18. Jahrhundert.
Lecture hall of the Faculty of Law in the 18th century.

Links: »Leipziger Studentengeographie« mit Empfehlungen für Bierlokale in umliegenden Dörfern.
Left: "Leipzig Students' Geography" with recommended ale-houses in the surrounding villages.

Das Georgenhaus am Brühl mit dem Frauenkolleg.
The Georgenhaus *on* Brühl *street with the* Frauenkolleg.

Dass die Universität so viele Studenten aus ärmeren Schichten anzieht, hat einen guten Grund: Viele versprechen sich in der Stadt des reichen Bürgertums, des Handels und Buchdrucks eine Möglichkeit zum Broterwerb. Und so entstehen die unterschiedlichsten Einkommensquellen: Manche Studenten arbeiten als so genannte Informatoren, das heißt, sie wirken in gut situierten Familien als Hauslehrer oder Erzieher. Andere sind Winkelschulhalter, sie geben gegen Gebühren Unterricht in den so genannten Winkelschulen, die betrieben werden, weil die Volksschulen der Stadt

VARIOUS WAYS OF EARNING A LIVING

Civil affluence was not only opposed by hard up craftsmen, but also by numerous impoverished students. Sometimes people would refer to the University as the "universitas pauperum", the academia of the poor. Statistically, the greatest number of impoverished students emanated from the Faculty of Theology, and the lowest number from the Faculty of Law. "Every day labourer lets his son study, if he can save him from starvation at school, and never gives a thought as to what he will survive on once he is at university",

Lithographie »Leipzig zu Goethes Studentenzeit 1765–1768«.
Lithograph "Leipzig in Goethe's student days 1765–1768".

Rechts: Begrüßung des Rektors durch Stadtsoldaten am Grimmaischen Tor.
Right: Welcome to the Rector by city soldiers at the Grimmaisches Tor.

Blick in den Karzer der Universität.
View of the detention room at the University.

in teilweise erbärmlichem Zustand sind. Theologiestudenten gehen an den Wochenenden Landgeistlichen oder Dorfküstern beim Gottesdienst zur Hand, andere sind als Musiker tätig, der Student Georg Philipp Telemann ruft das Collegium musicum ins Leben, wieder andere arbeiten als Korrektor in einem der zahlreichen Verlage. Stadtbekannt sind die so genannten Cicisbeos, die sich als Liebhaber oft älterer Damen ihr Geld verdienen, und schließlich müssen manche Studenten auch betteln gehen.

PARFÜMIERTE STUTZER

Doch es gibt auch Studenten, die sich durchaus etwas leisten können. Friedrich Wilhelm Zachariä beschreibt in »Der Rennomist – Ein scherzhaftes Heldengedicht« den typischen Leipziger Stutzer als einen, der »mit wohlgepudertem Schopf, in seidenen Strümpfen und Kleidern von Samt und Atlas einherläuft, nach Pomade und Parfüm duftet, seine ›Scharmante‹ umtänzelt und in puncto des Degens sehr friedfertigen Anschauungen huldigt«. Johann Wolfgang Goethe, der 1765 als 16-Jähriger zum Studium nach Leipzig kommt, erinnert sich an seine eigene Wandlung zum Stutzer. »Das erste, was die Frauen an mir tadelten, bezog sich auf die Kleidung, denn ich war von zu Hause freilich etwas wunderlich equipiert auf die Akademie gelangt«, heißt es in »Aus meinem Leben. Dichtung und Wahrheit«. Schließlich aber »faßte ich Mut und wagte, meine sämtliche Garderobe gegen eine neumodische, dem Ort gemäße, auf einmal umzutauschen, wodurch sie aber freilich sehr zusammenschrumpfte.« Dass Goethes neue Staffage eher spärlich ausfällt, dürfte

criticized Anselmus Rabiosus the Younger – his real name being Andreas Georg Friedrich Rebmann – in his work, *Wanderungen und Kreuzzüge durch einen Teil Deutschlands* ("Hikes and Crusades through a Part of Germany").

The reason the University attracted so many students from the lower classes was that many expected a city of commerce and printing, where so many rich citizens resided, would offer an opportunity to earn a better living. And thus various sources of income evolved: some students hired themselves out as so-called *Informatoren,* that is, tutors or educators. Others taught at *Winkelschulen* – they gave paid instruction in these schools that were instituted in order to compensate for the city's elementary schools, which were in a somewhat deplorable state. Theology students assisted rural clergymen or village sextons at church service at weekends. Some earned money as musicians, the student Georg Philipp Telemann called the Collegium musicum into being, and still others worked as proof-readers with one of the numerous publishing houses. The notorious Cicisbeos earned their living as lovers of, more often than not, elderly ladies. Finally, some students had to resort to beggary.

PERFUMED DANDIES

There were students, however, who were perfectly able to afford a comfortable lifestyle. Friedrich Wilhelm Zachariä described in *Der Rennomist – Ein scherzhaftes Heldengedicht* ("The Braggart – a Facetious Epic Poem") the typical Leipzig dandy as one who "walks around with well-powdered hair, in silk stockings and clothes of velvet and sateen, sweet with pomade and perfume, and tripping around his *Scharmante* (loved one) and paying homage to rather reserved views on the use of the rapier." Johann Wolfgang Goethe, who came as a 16-year-old to study in Leipzig in 1765, remembered his own transformation into a dandy. "The first thing that women would rebuke me for was my clothes, as I had arrived from home, and that is true, somewhat strangely equipped at the academy," he wrote in *Aus meinem Leben. Dichtung und Wahrheit* ("From my life: Poetry and Truth"). Finally however, "I took courage and dared to exchange all my clothes for new-fashioned ones, suitable to the place, admittedly, causing their number to shrink considerably."

daran liegen, dass die Kleidung der Leipziger Stutzer ziemlich teuer ist.

Unzufrieden zeigt sich Goethe mit seinem Studium. »Meine Collegia besuchte ich anfangs emsig und treulich; die Philosophie wollte mich jedoch keineswegs aufklären. In der Logik kam es mir wunderlich vor, daß ich diejenigen Geistesoperationen, die ich von Jugend auf mit der größten Bequemlichkeit verrichtete, so auseinanderzerren, vereinzelen und gleichsam zerstören sollte, um den rechten Gebrauch derselben einzusehen. Von dem Dinge, von der Welt, von Gott glaubte ich ungefähr soviel zu wissen als der Lehrer selbst, und es schien mir an mehr als einer Stelle gewaltig zu hapern«, schreibt er in »Dichtung und Wahrheit«. »Mit den juristischen Kollegien ward es bald ebenso schlimm, denn ich wußte gerade schon soviel, als uns der Lehrer zu überliefern für gut fand«, beklagt sich Goethe. Kein gutes Zeugnis, das er der Alma mater Lipsiensis ausstellt.

VERBLÜFFENDE VORSCHLÄGE

Dass es um die Hochschule nicht in allen Bereichen zum Besten steht, weiß man dort natürlich selbst. Zu Beginn des Jahrhunderts steht die Universität Leipzig im Ruf einer Provinzhochschule. Zum Teil weigern sich Fakultäten, bei der Neubesetzung von Lehrstühlen auch Bewerber von außerhalb zu berücksichtigen. Da teilweise in patriarchalischer Manier der Sohn dem Vater folgt, gibt es regelrechte Professorendynastien. Als die Mängel im Jahr 1711 allzu deutlich werden, soll eine Umfrage unter den Hochschullehrern Abhilfe

That Goethe's new wardrobe turned out to be rather sparse, might have been due to the fact that a dandy's clothes were quite expensive in Leipzig.

Goethe appeared to be dissatisfied with his studies. "Initially, I diligently and faithfully went to my courses; philosophy, however, would by no means enlighten me. In logic, it seemed strange to me that I was to tear apart, isolate and more or less destroy those mental operations that I had done from adolescence with the greatest ease in order to understand the right use of the same. I believed I knew as much as the teacher, of the thing, of the world, of God, and there seemed to be considerable weak points in more than one place," he wrote in *Dichtung und Wahrheit* ("Poetry and Truth"). "It was just as bad with the legal collegia, as I knew as much as the teacher found appropriate to pass on to us," Goethe complained. This did not reflect well on the Alma mater Lipsiensis.

STUNNING SUGGESTIONS

The academia at the University of Leipzig itself knew that it had not the best reputation in all areas. The University was reputed to be provincial at the beginning of the century. Faculties at times refused to consider applicants from outside Leipzig when vacant chairs needed to be filled. There were downright patriarchal dynasties, as a son could inherit his father's chair. When the shortcomings became all too obvious in 1711, a survey among the University lecturers was to remedy the situation. The suggestions for improvement were at times stunning: one professor called for

Johann Sebastian Bach, Thomaskantor und Komponist im Auftrag der Universität.
Johann Sebastian Bach, Cantor at St. Thomas Church and composer on behalf of the University.

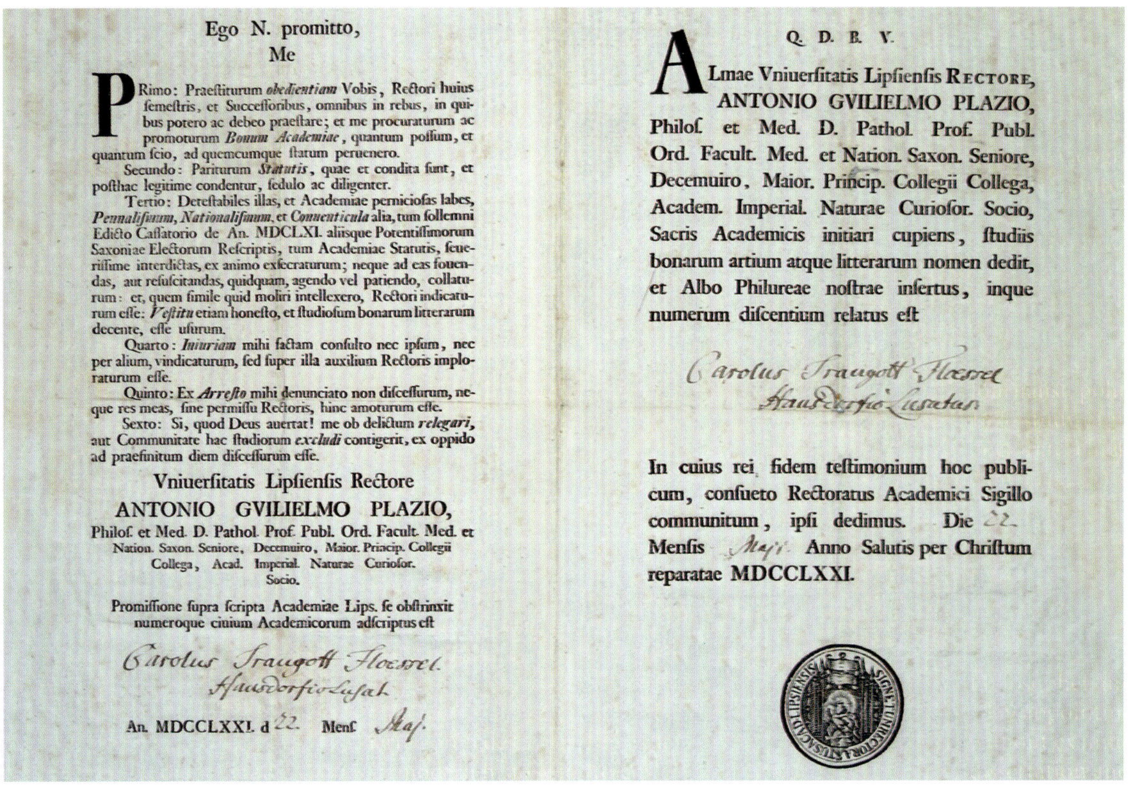

Ego N. promitto,
Me

PRimo: Praeſtiturum *obedientiam* Vobis, Rectori huius ſemeſtris, et Succeſſoribus, omnibus in rebus, in quibus potero ac debeo praeſtare; et me procuraturum ac promoturum *Bonum Academiae*, quantum poſſum, et quantum ſcio, ad quemcumque ſtatum peruenero.

Secundo: Pariturum *Statutis*, quae et condita ſunt, et poſthac legitime condentur, ſedulo ac diligenter.

Tertio: Deteſtabiles illas, et Academiae perniciofas labes, *Pennaliſmum, Nationaliſmum*, et *Conuenticula* alia, tum ſollemni Edicto Caſſatorio de An. MDCLXI. aliisque Potentiſſimorum Saxoniae Electorum Reſcriptis, tum Academiae Statutis, ſeueriſſime interdictas, ex animo exſecraturum; neque ad eas fouendas, aut reſuſcitandas, quidquam, agendo vel patiendo, collaturum: et, quem ſimile quid moliri intellexero, Rectori indicaturum eſſe: *Veſtitu* etiam honeſto, et ſtudioſum bonarum litterarum decente, eſſe uſurum.

Quarto: *Iniuriam* mihi factam conſulto nec ipſum, nec per alium, vindicaturum, ſed ſuper illa auxilium Rectoris imploraturum eſſe.

Quinto: Ex *Arreſto* mihi denunciato non diſceſſurum, neque res meas, ſine permiſſu Rectoris, hinc amoturum eſſe.

Sexto: Si, quod Deus auertat! me ob delictum *relegari*, aut Communitate hac ſtudiorum *excludi* contigerit, ex oppido ad praefinitum diem diſceſſurum eſſe.

Vniuerſitatis Lipſienſis Rectore
ANTONIO GVILIELMO PLAZIO,
Philoſ. et Med. D. Pathol. Prof. Publ. Ord. Facult. Med. et Nation. Saxon. Seniore, Decemuiro, Maior. Princip. Collegii Collega, Acad. Imperial. Naturae Curioſor. Socio.

Promiſſione ſupra ſcripta Academiae Lips. ſe obſtrinxit numeroque ciuium Academicorum adſcriptus eſt

Carolus Traugott Floessel.
Hausdorfio Lusat.

An. MDCCLXXI. d 22. Menſ. Maj.

Q. D. B. V.

ALmae Vniuerſitatis Lipſienſis RECTORE,
ANTONIO GVILIELMO PLAZIO,
Philoſ. et Med. D. Pathol. Prof. Publ. Ord. Facult. Med. et Nation. Saxon. Seniore, Decemuiro, Maior. Princip. Collegii Collega, Academ. Imperial. Naturae Curioſor. Socio, Sacris Academicis initiari cupiens, ſtudiis bonarum artium atque litterarum nomen dedit, et Albo Philureae noſtrae inſertus, inque numerum diſcentium relatus eſt

Carolus Traugott Floessel
Hausdorfio Lusatus

In cuius rei fidem teſtimonium hoc publicum, conſueto Rectoratus Academici Sigillo communitum, ipſi dedimus. Die 22. Menſis Maji Anno Salutis per Chriſtum reparatae MDCCLXXI.

Immatrikulationsurkunde mit Rektorsiegel vom 22. Mai 1771.
Certificate of enrolment with Rector's seal of 22 May 1771.

Kreuzgang der Universitätskirche St. Pauli.
Cloister of the University Church St. Pauli.

Prominente Studenten des 18. Jahrhunderts: Klopstock, Seume, Jean Paul, Lessing und Novalis (von links).
Students of note during the 18th century : Klopstock, Seume, Jean Paul, Lessing and Novalis (from left).

schaffen. Die Verbesserungsvorschläge sind zum Teil verblüffend: Da fordert ein Professor die Lockerung des Duellverbots, ein anderer glaubt, durch das Angebot einer Reitschule könne die Universität wieder attraktiver werden. Von anderer Stelle wird die Beschäftigung eines französischen Tanzlehrers gefordert und schließlich soll es an allen Fakultäten so genannte Winterauditorien geben, weil es im Winter für den Professor zu beschwerlich sei, seine Stunden abzuhalten, und für die Studenten sogar unmöglich, daran teilzunehmen.

Tatsächlich werden im 18. Jahrhundert die Einrichtungen für Forschung und Lehre zum Teil erweitert, allerdings nicht im Sinne der Professoren von 1711. So entsteht zum Beispiel im Turm der Pleißenburg in den 1790er-Jahren die Sternwarte, deren erster Observator, der außerordentliche Professor Christian Friedrich Rüdiger, das »Handbuch der rechnenden Astronomie« verfasste. In enger Zusammenarbeit mit der Stadt richtet die Universität zudem ein klinisches Institut am städtischen Hospital St. Jakob ein. Erstmals führt hier am 29. April 1799 der Mediziner Ernst Platner Unterweisungen direkt am Krankenbett durch.

the ban on duels to be eased, another one believed the University might become more attractive again if it were to establish a riding school. Still another proposed hiring a French dance master and, finally, there was the suggestion to set up so-called winter lecture halls at all faculties, as it would be too ardous for the professor to deliver his hours in winter, and even impossible for the students to attend.

Facilities for research and teaching were actually partly expanded in the 18th century, but, not as a result of any of the suggestions offered by the professors during the year 1711. For instance, the observatory was opened in the tower of the *Pleißenburg* in the 1790s, the first observator of which, the associate professor Christian Friedrich Rüdiger, wrote the *Handbuch der rechnenden Astronomie* ("Guide to the Calculating Astronomy"). Furthermore, in close cooperation with the city, the University set up a clinical institute at the St. Jacob municipal hospital. The physician, Ernst Platner, gave instructions right at the patients' bedside for the first time on 29 April 1799.

Studentische Abendmusik 1783 in der Grimmaischen Straße.
Student soiree in Grimmaische Straße *in 1783.*

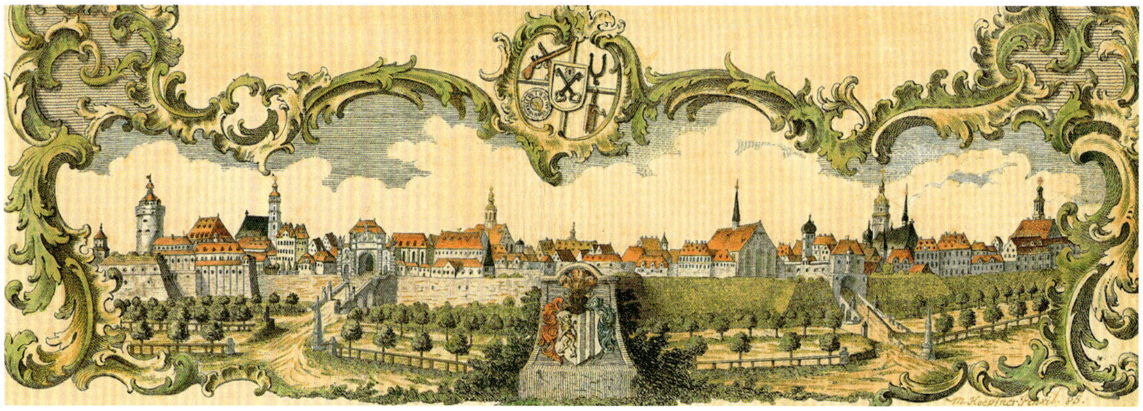

Leipzig 1785 von Osten aus gesehen.
Leipzig seen from the east in 1785.

ZAHLREICHE HOCHSCHULEN

Zum Ende des 18. Jahrhunderts ist die Alma mater Lipsiensis eine von insgesamt 43 Universitäten im deutschsprachigen Raum. Zum Teil hatten kleine Landesfürsten aus einer Laune heraus Hochschulen gegründet, die nun um die Gunst der Studenten buhlen. Insgesamt geht die Zahl der Studierenden stark zurück, manche kleine Einrichtung bringt es auf gerade einmal 200 Studenten. Die Leipziger Universität liegt mit rund 400 eingeschriebenen Studierenden hinter Halle mit 730 und Göttingen mit 660 in der Gruppe der größeren Hochschulen. An der Universität lehren zur Jahrhundertwende 58 ordentliche und außerordentliche Professoren, eine für die damalige Zeit große Zahl. Sie ist auch Voraussetzung dafür, dass die Leipziger Universität zu herausragenden wissenschaftlichen Leistungen ansetzen kann.

Das Siegel der Juristischen Fakultät.
The seal of the Faculty of Law.

NUMEROUS UNIVERSITIES

Towards the end of the 18th century, the Alma mater Lipsiensis was one of 43 universities in the German-speaking areas. At times, regional sovereigns had spontaneously founded institutions of higher academic learning, which now courted the students' favour. This resulted in a considerable decline of student enrolments – some institutions numbered no more than 200 students. The University of Leipzig had approximately 430 students, whereas Halle had 730 and Göttingen had 660 students, respectively. All three were considered to be the larger universities. At the turn of the century, 58 full and associate professors were teaching at the University, which was a significant number for that time. This size would enable the University to achieve outstanding scientific results.

Pleißenburg mit 1794 im Turm eröffneter Universitätssternwarte.
Pleißenburg *castle and University observatory, opened in the tower in 1794.*

DAS 18. JAHRHUNDERT
THE 18TH CENTURY

BLICK IN DIE WELT
VIEW OF THE WORLD

1701 Preußen wird Königreich und steigt zur europäischen Großmacht auf. Prussia becomes a kingdom and ascends toward a great European power.

1703 Zar Peter der Große gründet Sankt Petersburg und erklärt es zur russischen Hauptstadt. Tsar Peter the Great founds St. Petersburg and declares it the Russian capital.

1707 England und Schottland schließen sich zum Königreich Großbritannien zusammen. England and Scotland unite to form the Kingdom of Great Britain.

1718 Franzosen bauen die später New Orleans genannte Stadt am Mississippi. The French build the city on the Mississippi, which will later be called New Orleans.

1725 Antonio Vivaldi veröffentlicht seine Komposition »Die vier Jahreszeiten«. Antonio Vivaldi publishes his composition, "The Four Seasons".

1746 Voltaire popularisiert in seinen Philosophischen Erzählungen die Gedanken der Aufklärung. Voltaire popularizes the ideas of enlightenment in his philosophical accounts.

1752 Benjamin Franklin erfindet in Boston den Blitzableiter. Benjamin Franklin invents the lightning rod in Boston.

1755 Ein großes Erdbeben zerstört Lissabon und fordert 30 000 Menschenleben. A heavy earthquake destroys Lisboa and claims 30,000 lives.

1756 Friedrich der Große beginnt den Siebenjährigen Krieg. Frederick the Great starts the Seven Years' War.

1769 James Watt legt mit seiner Dampfmaschine den Grundstein für die industrielle Revolution. James Watt lays the foundation for the Industrial Revolution with his steam engine.

1776 Thomas Jefferson verfasst die amerikanische Unabhängigkeitserklärung. Thomas Jefferson writes the United States Declaration of Independence.

1789 Die Französische Revolution beginnt mit dem Sturm auf die Bastille. The Storming of the Bastille marks the beginning of the French Revolution.

1790 Wolfgang Amadeus Mozart schreibt in Wien seine Oper »Die Zauberflöte«. Wolfgang Amadeus Mozart writes his opera "The Magic Flute" in Vienna.

BERÜHMTHEITEN AN DER UNIVERSITÄT
ILLUSTRIOUS PEOPLE AT THE UNIVERSITY

Christian Fürchtegott Gellert 1715–1769
Volksdichter, Philosoph, Sprachlehrer und Aufklärer, hält ab 1745 stets überfüllte Vorlesungen zu Poesie, Beredsamkeit und Moral. Popular poet, philosopher, language teacher and proponent of the enlightenment, lectured in poetry, eloquence and morals, in overcrowded lecture halls, from 1745.

Christian Wolff 1679–1754
Philosoph und Universalgelehrter, ab 1703 Hochschullehrer und zeitweise Prediger in Leipzig, definiert zahlreiche Grundbegriffe der deutschen Philosophie. Philosopher and polymath, from 1703 professor and temporarily preacher in Leipzig, defined many fundamental terms of German philosophy.

Johann Adam Hiller 1728–1804
Dirigent, Komponist und Musiktheoretiker, 1751 bis 1754 Jurastudium in Leipzig, 1781 erster Gewandhauskapellmeister, 1789 bis 1801 Thomaskantor. Conductor, composer and music theorist, 1751 to 1754 law studies in Leipzig, 1781 first *Gewandhaus* music director, 1789 to 1801 Cantor at St. Thomas Church.

Johann Gottlieb Fichte 1762–1814
Philosoph, Erzieher und bedeutender Vertreter des deutschen Idealismus, von 1781 bis 1784 Theologiestudium an der Universität, danach Privatlehrer in Leipzig. Philosopher, educator and important exponent of German idealism, from 1781 to 1784 study of theology at the University, then private teacher in Leipzig.

Georg Philipp Telemann 1681–1767
Komponist und Musiker, ab 1701 Jurastudium, 1703 Gründer und Leiter des studentischen Collegium musicum, 1704 Organist und Musikdirektor an der Neukirche. Composer and musician, from 1701 law studies, 1703 founder and director of the student Collegium musicum, 1704 organist and music director at the Neukirche.

Die Universität im 19. Jahrhundert The University in the 19th Century

ZIGARREN, REVOLUTIONEN UND EINE REGE BAUTÄTIGKEIT
CIGARS, REVOLUTIONS AND BUSTLE OF BUILDING ACTIVITIES

Der Aufstand der Franzosen und ihre demokratischen Forderungen nach »Freiheit – Gleichheit – Brüderlichkeit« werden im ausgehenden 18. Jahrhundert in Leipzig und der Universität interessiert wahrgenommen. Teile des Bürgertums und der Intelligenz sympathisieren mit den neuen Ideen. Manch einer erkennt Parallelen zwischen der vorrevolutionären Situation in Frankreich und der absolutistischen Herrschaft im Kurfürstentum Sachsen. An der Universität äußert der Philosoph Friedrich Gottlob Born öffentlich seine Sympathie für die neuen Verhältnisse in Frankreich. Die Herrschenden reagieren mit Untersuchungen gegen Born, die aber lediglich in einer Geldbuße münden. Als gegen den Philologen Johann Friedrich Hilscher ein Verfahren wegen kritischer Äußerungen eingeleitet wird, emigriert er.

Während in Sachsen ein Umbruch nach französischem Vorbild vorerst ausbleibt, werden an der Universität Neuerungen eingeführt, die für sich das Prädikat »revolutionär« in Anspruch nehmen dürfen. Die Aufklärer des 18. Jahrhunderts haben Ideen entwickelt, mit denen sie Erziehung und Bildung auf neue Wege führen. Bisher herrschte allein die alte, scholastische Form der Lehre: In den Vorlesungen haben die Studenten zuzuhören, höchstens bei einfachen Übungen können sie aktiv werden.

The uprising of the French and their democratic call for "Liberty – Equality – Fraternity" were perceived with intrigue by Leipzig and the University at the end of the 18th century. Some of the bourgeoisie and the intelligentsia sympathized with the new ideas. Many recognized parallels between the pre-revolutionary situation in France and the absolutist rule in the Electorate of Saxony. At the University the philosopher Friedrich Gottlob Born openly expressed his sympathy for the new situation in France. The rulers reacted by launching investigations against Born, which ultimately resulted in a fine. When proceedings began against the philologist Johann Friedrich Hilscher, because of his critical statements, he emigrated.

In Saxony a transition to the French model failed to materialize, but the University introduced changes which may well have claimed the rating of "revolutionary". The proponents of enlightenment of the 18th century had developed ideas that would break new ground for education and training. Up to that point, the old way of scholastic teaching had been in existence: students had to listen during lectures, at the most they might have been able to become actively involved in simple exercises.

Aphrodite im 1836 gegründeten Antikenmuseum der Universität.
Aphrodite in the Antiques Museum of the University founded in 1836.

Heutiger Lesesaal in der Ende des 19. Jahrhunderts von Arwed Roßbach erbauten Bibliotheca Albertina.
Today's reading room in the Bibliotheca Albertina built by Arwed Rossbach at the end of the 19th century.

Theodor Körner, Jurastudent und Verfasser des Liedes »Lützows wilde verwegene Jagd«.
Theodor Körner, law student and author of the song "Lützows wild and bold hunt".

SEMINARE STATT SCHOLASTIK

Dass nun die Studenten den Lernprozess gemeinsam mit den Lehrenden gestalten, ist wahrhaft umwälzend. Antrieb geben hierbei vor allem der Philosophie-Professor Christian Daniel Beck (1757–1832) und der Philologe Gottfried Hermann (1772–1848). Beck gründet um die Jahrhundertwende eine »Philologische Gesellschaft«, in der Studenten unter Anleitung der Professoren die Spezifik der Sprachen kennen lernen. Und von Hermanns »Societas graeca« geht die Entfaltung hin zu mehr Eigenaktivität der Studierenden aus. Dies mündet schließlich in die so genannten Seminare. Neben der Verankerung der Pädagogik als Universitätsdisziplin ist deren Bildung ein bedeutender Schritt zur Verbesserung der Lehrtätigkeit.

Gleichwohl sind die Lehrveranstaltungen nicht mit modernen Seminaren vergleichbar. Professoren stehen im Ruf der Respektsperson und des Unikums gleichermaßen. So etwa der Jurist Bernhard Windscheid (1817–1892), der seinen Studenten das Zigarrerauchen im Hörsaal untersagt, da ihn der Geruch störe. Als einige munter weiterpaffen, fertigt er die Frevler ab: »Ich hatte Sie, meine Herren, das letzte Mal gebeten, das Rauchen im Saale vor meiner Vorlesung zu unterlassen; ich sehe, Sie sind außerstande, meiner Bitte zu entsprechen, ich schränke sie deshalb dahin ein, rauchen Sie wenigstens bessere Zigarren!« Donnerndes Getrampel ist die Antwort – und keiner greift fortan mehr zum Tabak.

Ein anderer Professor hat eine feuchte Aussprache, wie ein Student berichtet: »Er sprudelte, indem er sprach, so lebhaft, daß er das Papier, auf dem man nachschreiben wollte, feucht machte. Es kam wohl vor, daß die Betroffenen einen roten Regenschirm aufspannten, um unter dessen Schutz ruhig schreiben zu können; er ließ sich das gern gefallen.«

SEMINARS INSTEAD OF SCHOLASTICISM

That students should now design the learning process together with the lecturers was truly a sweeping change, the driving forces behind which were mainly the philosophy professor Christian Daniel Beck (1757–1832) and the philologist Gottfried Hermann (1772–1848). Beck founded a "Philological Society" around the turn of the century, where students got to know the specifics of languages under professorial guidance. And from Hermann's "Societas graeca" unfolded greater self-initiative on the part of the students. This finally resulted in the so-called seminars. In addition to the entrenchment of pedagogy as a university discipline, its development was an important step towards the improvement of teaching.

Nevertheless, courses were by no means comparable to modern seminars. A professor enjoyed the reputation of being both a person to be respected and an original character, such as the jurist Bernhard Windscheid (1817–1892), who prohibited his students from smoking cigars in the lecture hall as the smell disturbed him. While some happily continued to puff away, he dealt with the malefactors: "Last time, I had asked you, gentlemen, to refrain from smoking in the lecture hall before my lecture; I see you are unable to comply with my request, therefore, I will reduce it to the following – smoke better cigars at least!" There was a thundering reply and thereupon nobody ever resorted to tobacco again.

Another professor spattered when he spoke, as one student reported. "When speaking, he kept gushing in such a lively manner as to wet the paper you wanted to write on. It might well have happened that those concerned would have opened a red umbrella in order to be able to quietly write in its shelter. He would readily put up with it."

Tumulte im Jahr 1830 am Freudenhaus.
Riots at the brothel in 1830.

Postkarte mit alten Universitätsgebäuden aus der Mitte des 19. Jahrhunderts.
Postcard showing old University buildings from the mid 19th century.

INSTITUTE UND STIFTUNGEN

Neue Formen der Wissensvermittlung werden in vielen Fällen von der Gründung neuer Institute begleitet. So führt die Einrichtung des Klinischen Instituts im städtischen Krankenhaus St. Jakob 1812 zur Schaffung der ordentlichen Professur »Klinik«. Direkt am Krankenbett erleben die angehenden Mediziner in ihrer Ausbildung praktische Elemente der Behandlung und Pflege von Patienten. Sie sind bei Untersuchungen dabei, sehen chirurgische Eingriffe und sammeln Erfahrungen bei Sezierübungen. Die bis dahin überwiegend theoretisch orientierte Ausbildung erhält eine praktische Ergänzung.

So wie auch andere Fakultäten profitieren die Mediziner von Stiftungen. Im Jahr 1810 ermöglichen es Mittel der Trierschen Stiftung, eine Gynäkologische Klinik einzurichten, der eine Schule zur Ausbildung von Hebammen angeschlossen ist. Dort lehrt und forscht Johann Gottfried Jörg (1779 – 1856), der die Gynäkologie zu einem eigenständigen Fachgebiet an der Medizinischen Fakultät macht. Am 1. Juni 1820 gründet Friedrich Philipp Ritterich (1782 – 1866) eine »Heilanstalt für arme Augenkranke« und legt den Grundstock für die Entwicklung der Augenheilkunde zum Universitätsfach.

Auch in der Physik beschäftigen sich die Wissenschaftler mit neuen Teildisziplinen, so Christian Samuel Weiß (1780 – 1856), der ein geometrisches System der Kristallographie entwickelt. Georg Heinrich Borz (1714 – 1799) entdeckt bisher unbekannte Gebiete der Hydrodynamik und der Optik, Gustav Theodor Fechner (1801 – 1887) hält ab 1824 Vorlesungen über Galvanismus, Elektrizität, Elektromagnetismus und

INSTITUTES AND FOUNDATIONS

New forms of knowledge transfer were often accompanied by the foundation of new institutes. The establishment of the Clinical Institute within the St. Jacob municipal hospital in 1812 resulted in the creation of a full professorship "clinic". Doctors-to-be oversaw practical elements of patient treatment and care right at the patient's bedside during their training. They participated in medical examinations, witnessed surgical interventions and gained experience in dissection

Barrikadenkämpfe 1848 in der Grimmaischen Straße.
Street battles in the Grimmaische Straße *in 1848.*

Ehrenfahnen-Übergabe an Leipzigs Studenten am 31. Oktober 1830.
Handover of the Flag of Honour to the students of Leipzig on 31 October 1830.

Elektrochemie. Fechner wie der Mathematiker August Ferdinand Möbius öffnen ihre Universitätsvorträge für ein breites bürgerliches Publikum.

STUDENTISCHE KORPORATIONEN

Aber nicht nur die Lehrmethoden verändern sich, auch das studentische Miteinander findet neue Ausdrucksformen. Unter dem Eindruck der Französischen Revolution verbreiten sich in Deutschland die Ideen des Liberalismus und Nationalismus. Um 1810 entwerfen Friedrich Friesen, Friedrich Ludwig Jahn und andere Schüler Johann Gottlieb Fichtes den Plan einer Deutschen Burschenschaft. Diese soll das Volk und die Verantwortung des Einzelnen gegenüber dem Ganzen in den Mittelpunkt des studentischen Lebens stellen und wertet die Volksgemeinschaft höher als Landesherrschaft und Standesunterschiede. Das politische Engagement findet seinen Ausdruck in dem Wahlspruch »Freiheit – Ehre – Vaterland«.

exercises. The rather theoretically oriented education of the day was completed with a practical component.

Physicians benefited from the assistance of foundations, as other faculties did. In 1810, endowments from the *Triersche* Foundation enabled the setup of a gynaecological clinic, with an affiliated school of midwifery. This was the place of teaching and research of Johann Gottfried Jörg (1779 – 1856) who made gynaecology an independent field at the Faculty of Medicine. On 1 June 1820, Friedrich Philipp Ritterich (1782 – 1866) founded a hospital for "poor ophthalmics" and paved the way for the development of ophthalmology to become a university subject.

Scientists engaged in new sub-disciplines in physics as well, such as Christian Samuel Weiß (1780 – 1856) who developed a geometrical system of cristallography. Georg Heinrich Borz (1714 – 1799) discovered previously unknown fields of hydrodynamics and optics. Gustav Theodor Fechner (1801 – 1887) lectured in galvanism, electricity, electromagnetism and

Wappen der studentischen Korporationen.
Crests of the student corporations.

Rechts: Burschenschafter in bierseliger Runde.
Right: Fraternists in a boozy setting.

Die Burschenschaften wollen die nationale Zerrissenheit des deutschen Volkes überwinden. Sie erweisen sich als Träger der fortschrittlichen demokratischen Ideen und erhalten Zulauf. Das macht sie aus Sicht des Staates gefährlich. Seit 1815 gehört Sachsen zum Deutschen Bund. König Friedrich August I. folgt den Entscheidungen des Bundes. Und der erklärt die Burschenschaften für illegal. Im Dezember 1820 ereilt die Leipziger Burschenschaft das Verbot, das 1832 auf alle politischen Vereine und Versammlungen, Fahnen und Abzeichen, Feste und Reden erweitert wird.

Der Deutsche Bund entscheidet, die Staatsaufsicht wegen der »Umtriebe« an deutschen Universitäten zu verstärken. So wird ein Beauftragter eingesetzt, der die bis dahin wohlwollend-lockere Oberaufsicht des Staates strafft. Gleichzeitig wird die Förderung der

electrochemistry from 1824. Both Fechner and the mathematician August Ferdinand Möbius opened their university presentations to a large civil public.

STUDENT CORPORATIONS

Not only teaching methods changed, but also student interaction found new ways of expression. The ideas of liberalism and nationalism spread in Germany under the impact of the French Revolution. In about 1810, Friedrich Friesen, Friedrich Ludwig Jahn and other students of Johann Gottlieb Fichte drafted the plan for a German Fraternity. Student life was to focus on the people and the responsibility of the individual to the common good. Community and the nation as a whole were rated higher than territorial lordship or class distinctions. This political engagement manifested in the slogan "Liberty – Honour – Fatherland".

The fraternities wanted to overcome disruption of the German nation and were proven to carry progressive democratic ideas. They enjoyed a large following. This made them dangerous from the state's perspective. Since 1815 Saxony had been part of the German Confederation. King Frederick Augustus I followed the decisions of the Confederation which declared the fraternities to be illegal. The ban which overtook the Leipzig fraternity in December 1820 would be extended to all political associations and assemblies, flags and badges, festivals and speeches. The German Confederation decided to strengthen state supervision because of "activities" at German universities. A representative was put in charge in order to tighten the rather laid back state supervision. At the same time, promotion of the University was enhanced. For instance, there was a state grant of 4,000 *Reichstaler* from 1825 and the University library received 400 *Reichstaler* annually. The extension of academic potential, however, went hand in hand with a growing influence of the state.

That influence brought about another reform of the University. The Alma mater was given a new constitution in 1830, the main components of which were: the end of medieval jurisdiction; the public appointment procedure for professors; the reorganization of finances; the creation of an Academic Senate chaired by the Rector, who was now to be elected

Die 1855 geschaffene und 1909 um zwei Bildnisse erweiterte Rektorkette.
Rector's chain of office, created in 1855 and extended by two portraits in 1909.

Links: Frühstücksbude im Paulinerhof.
Left: Breakfast stall in Paulinerhof.

Studenten bei der Mensur.
Students' fencing duel.

Das Paulinum um 1830.
The Paulinum around 1830.

Rechts: Das 1836 eröffnete neue Hauptgebäude am Augustusplatz.
Right: The main bulding at Augustusplatz *square, opened in 1836.*

Universität verbessert. So gibt es ab 1825 einen staatlichen Zuschuss von 4 000 Reichstalern, die Universitätsbibliothek erhält 400 Reichstaler jährlich. Der Ausbau der wissenschaftlichen Leistungsfähigkeit geht jedoch mit einer wachsenden Einflussnahme des Staates einher.

Dieser Einfluss führt zur zweiten Reform der Universität: Die Alma mater erhält 1830 eine neue Verfassung, deren wesentliche Bestandteile der Wegfall der mittelalterlichen Gerichtsbarkeit, die öffentlichen Berufungsverfahren der Professuren, die Neuordnung der Finanzen, die Schaffung eines Akademischen Senats unter Vorsitz des nun jährlich zu bestimmenden Rektors und grundlegende Veränderungen der Nationen-Strukturen und der Lehrinhalte sind. Befördert wird die Reform von dem Philosophen Wilhelm Traugott Krug, der 1809 aus Königsberg nach Leipzig gekommen ist. Er wird 1813 und 1830 Rektor.

GÖTTINGER SIEBEN

1837 erschüttert ein politischer Skandal das Bürgertum. Der hannoversche Monarch setzt die Staatsverfassung in seinem Königreich außer Kraft. In einer »Protestation des Gewissens« verurteilen sieben Göttinger Professoren den Staatsstreich – und werden ihrer Ämter enthoben. Zwei von ihnen finden an der Leipziger Universität eine neue Anstellung: Der Rechtshistoriker

annually; and essential changes to nation structures and course content. This reform was advanced by the philosopher Wilhelm Traugott Krug, who had come from Königsberg to Leipzig in 1809. He would become Rector in 1813 and 1830.

THE GÖTTINGEN SEVEN

In 1837 a political scandal shook the bourgeoisie. The Monarch of Hanover annulled the state constitution in his kingdom. In a "Protestation of Conscience", seven professors from Göttingen condemned this coup and were relieved of their positions at the university. Two of them found new employment at the University of Leipzig: law historian Wilhelm Eduard Albrecht was allowed to teach in Leipzig from 1838 and was appointed full professor at the Faculty of Law in 1840; and in 1843 the physicist Wilhelm Eduard Weber was another professor from Göttingen to be salaried in Leipzig.

Only a short time later, revolution seized the German Confederation. The revolutionaries wanted a democratic and nationally unified state. Toward the end of the "March Revolution" in 1848/49, they attempted to overthrow King Frederick Augustus II in Saxony. Also Leipzig students sprang to arms, but the rebellion was put down with the help of Prussia and

Leipziger Stadtansicht um 1860 mit Pleißenburg, Bürgerschule auf der Moritzbastei, Bildermuseum, Augusteum, Paulinerkirche und Universitätsgebäuden im »lateinischen Viertel« (von links nach rechts).
City view of Leipzig around 1860, showing Pleißenburg *castle, secondary school at* Moritzbastei, *Museum of Fine Arts, Augusteum,* Pauliner *Church and University buildings in the "latin quarter" (from left to right).*

Augusteum und Paulinerkirche am Ende des 19. Jahrhunderts.
Augusteum and Pauliner Church at the end of the 19th century.

Wilhelm Eduard Albrecht darf ab 1838 in Leipzig lehren und wird 1840 zum ordentlichen Professor an der Juristenfakultät berufen. 1843 wird mit dem Physiker Wilhelm Eduard Weber ein weiterer Professor aus Göttingen in Leipzig angestellt.

Nur wenig später erfasst die Revolution den Deutschen Bund. Die Revolutionäre wollen einen demokratischen und national einheitlichen Staat. Gegen Ende der Märzrevolution von 1848/49 versuchen sie in Sachsen, König Friedrich August II. zu stürzen. Auch Leipziger Studenten eilen zu den Waffen, der Aufstand wird mit preußischer Hilfe jedoch blutig niedergeschlagen. Die Leipziger Professoren Moritz Haupt, Otto Jahn und Theodor Mommsen, die den Aufstand unterstützen, teilen das Schicksal ihrer Göttinger Kollegen und werden entlassen.

DEUTSCHE SPITZE

Ungeachtet aller Unruhen gedeiht die Universität. Nach dem relativen Anteil der Wissenschaftsausgaben liegt Sachsen nun an zweiter Stelle hinter Baden. An der sächsischen Landesuniversität beginnt eine rege Bautätigkeit. 1844 wird ein chemisches Labor eingerichtet, 1861 die Sternwarte am Johannistal eingeweiht. 1871 wird ein pathologisch-anatomisches Institut neu gebaut, zwei Jahre später ein physikalisches Institut. 1878 entsteht die erste deutsche Wetterstation. Von 1887 bis 1891 wird die Universitätsbibliothek Bibliotheca Albertina errichtet.

involved bloodshed. The Leipzig professors Moritz Haupt, Otto Jahn and Theodor Mommsen, who supported the rebellion, shared the fate of their Göttingen colleagues and were dismissed.

TOP RANK IN GERMANY

Albeit all disturbances the University prospered. Saxony ranked second behind Baden as to the relative proportion of science expenditure. The bustle of building activities began at the Saxon State University: in 1844 a chemical laboratory was set up and in 1861 the observatory at *Johannistal* was inaugurated. In 1871 a

Gründung der Königlich Sächsischen Gesellschaft der Wissenschaften im Juli 1846 in der Universitätsaula.
Foundation of the Royal Saxon Academy of Sciences in the assembly hall of the University in July 1846.

Die bedeutenden Leipziger Professoren (von links) Wundt (Psychologie), Marchand (Pathologie), Zirkel (Mineralogie), Des Coudres (Physik), Bruns (Astronomie), Leskien (Slawistik), Pfeffer (Botanik), Sievers (Germanistik), Chun (Zoologie), Beckmann (Chemie), Boehm (Pharmazie), Guethe (Theologie), Binding (Jura) und Hantzsch (Chemie).
The Leipzig professors of note (from left) Wundt (Psychology), Marchand (Pathology), Zirkel (Mineralogy), Des Coudres (Physics), Bruns (Astronomy), Leskien (Slavonic studies), Pfeffer (Botany), Sievers (German studies), Chun (Zoology), Beckmann (Chemistry), Boehm (Pharmacy), Guethe (Theology), Binding (Law) und Hantzsch (Chemistry).

Kernstück aber ist der Bau funktionaler und repräsentativer Hauptgebäude am Augustusplatz. 1830 wird damit begonnen, die Zwingerbauten südlich der Paulinerkirche abzubrechen. Von 1831 bis 1836 errichtet Universitätsbaumeister Alfred Geutebrück das Augusteum, so benannt zu Ehren von König Friedrich August I. von Sachsen. Die Entwürfe von Geutebrück werden durch Vorschläge von Karl Friedrich Schinkel ergänzt, insbesondere die Fassadengestaltung und das Portal. Das Hauptgebäude verfügt über 840 Sitzplätze in neun Hörsälen. In drei Sälen des Augusteums findet die Universitätsbibliothek einige Zeit Platz für ihre rund 100 000 Bände und wertvollen Handschriften. Bis Anfang der 1870er-Jahre rückt Leipzig auf den zweiten Platz in der Studentenfrequenz vor, zwischen 1872 und 1878 steht die Hochschule sogar vor Berlin auf dem ersten Rang der deutschen Universitäten.

Album mit Professorenbildern aus dem Jahr 1874.
Album with professors' portraits from the year 1874.

SEMMELFRAU UND GOSE

Ganz in der Nähe des Augusteums finden Studenten das Büdchen der Semmelfrau. In seiner Abschiedsrede als Rektor zeichnet der Archäologieprofessor Johannes Overbeck (1826 – 1895) dessen Bild so: »Aber noch an einer anderen Stelle staute und drängte sich die Menge unserer Commilitonen je länger in um so bedenklicherer Weise, um die Frühstücksbude im

pathological-anatomical institute was newly built and a physical institute two years later. The first German weather station opened in 1878. From 1887 to 1891, the University library Bibliotheca Albertina was built.

The key element, however, was the construction of representative and functional main buildings at *Augustusplatz* square. The demolition of the ward buildings south of *Pauliner* Church began in 1830. From 1831 to 1836, the University's master-builder Alfred Geutebrück erected the Augusteum, named in honour of King Frederick Augustus I of Saxony. The drafts by Geutebrück were completed with suggestions from Karl Friedrich Schinkel for the design of the façade and the portal in particular. The main building had 840 seats in nine lecture halls. The University library found shelter for its approximately 100,000 volumes and valuable manuscripts in three halls of the Augusteum for some time. Until the beginning of the 1870's, Leipzig advanced to the second position for student attendance. The University ranked first among German universities before Berlin between 1872 and 1878.

BUN WOMAN AND GOSE BEER

Students found the bun woman's stall very close to the Augusteum. Archeology professor Johannes Overbeck (1826 – 1895), in his farewell address as Rector, described it like this: "But it was into another place that the host of our fellow students crowded, the longer the lines the more alarming, at the breakfast stall in

Senatssaal, Aula und Wandelhalle im 1897 umgebauten Augusteum.
Senate hall, assembly hall and gallery in the Augusteum revamped in 1897.

Seitengange des Pauliner Kreuzganges.« Die Frühstücksbude geht auf die Frau mit dem Semmelkorb zurück, die die Hungernden versorgt. 1868 »musste die Semmelfrau in den Seitengang weichen, wo ihr ein Büdchen angewiesen wurde, aus dem sie nicht mehr nur belegte und unbelegte Semmeln, sondern mancherlei andere gute Dinge, Kuchen und Obst, Bouillon und Eier, verabreichte«.

Über eines der Lieblingsgetränke der Studenten geben verschiedene Dokumente Auskunft. So heißt es in einer Festschrift: »Die Gose wird in hiesiger Gegend überall ausgeschenkt, besonders in den bekannten Gosenschänken von Leipzig und Halle. Bewegte Stunden frohen Studentenlebens sind in diesen Gaststätten vorübergezogen, und mancher Philister in hohen Semestern hat von dieser guten Übung seiner jungen Jahre nicht abgelassen.« Die Studenten allerdings übertreiben es bisweilen mit der Übung: In der von Heinrich Martin Cajeri 1859 eröffneten Gosenschänke gilt das »Abtragen« von Studenten, die dem obergärigen Weißbier übermäßig zugesprochen haben, als Attraktion: »Man transportierte sie auf der hölzernen Trage, mit der die Gose aus dem Keller geholt wurde, zur Pleiße und kippte sie in das klare knietiefe Wasser.«

Flasche für die nicht nur bei Studenten beliebte Leipziger Gose.
Bottle for the Gose beer, not only popular with students.

the lateral passage of the Pauliner cloister." The breakfast stall dated back to the woman with the bun basket, who provided food for those who were starving. In 1868 "the bun woman had to move to the lateral passage where she was assigned a small stall, from which she would not only provide open-faced and plain buns, but a variety of other good things, cake and fruit, bouillon and eggs."

Several documents informed about one of the students' favourite drinks. A memorial publication read for instance, "The Gose is served everywhere in this region, especially in the well known Gose inns of Leipzig and Halle. Students spent many a happy hour in those inns. Many a Philistine in his elder semester has not surceased this good exercise of his younger years." Students, however, went overboard in this exercise at times though. The "removal" of students who had excessively enjoyed their top-fermented wheat beer was considered an attraction in the Gose inn opened by Heinrich Martin Cajeri in 1859: "They were transported to the *Pleiße* river on a wooden stretcher, on which one would also fetch the Gose from the cellar, and then were dumped into the clear knee deep water."

Die 1891 eröffnete Universitätsbibliothek im Musikviertel. *The University library, opened in 1891 in the Music Quarter.*

Die 1861 eröffnete Sternwarte im Johannistal.
The observatory in Johannistal, *opened in 1861.*

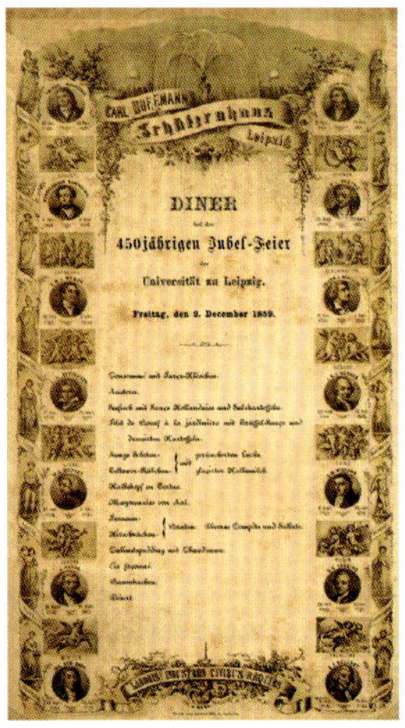

Menükarte zum 450-jährigen Gründungsjubiläum.
Menu of the 450th anniversary of the foundation.

ERSTE MEDIZINERIN

Ende des Jahrhunderts vollzieht sich an der Leipziger Universität eine weitere Revolution: 1880 legt die Engländerin Hope Bridge Adams als erste Frau an einer deutschen Universität das medizinische Staatsexamen ab. Und das zu einer Zeit, in der die Immatrikulation von weiblichen Studienbewerbern undenkbar ist. Das mag auch der Grund dafür sein, dass die Medizinische Fakultät ihr zwar das Staatsexamen ermöglicht, eine Promotion jedoch verwehrt. Wenige Jahre zuvor hatten auch die Juristen eine Frau zu Prüfungen zugelassen, 1873 kann eine Russin sogar promovieren.

Der Wandel Sachsens vom Agrar- zum Industrieland im letzten Drittel des 19. Jahrhunderts wird in der sich stark differenzierenden Fächervielfalt an der Universität Leipzig deutlich sichtbar. Der Chemiker Hermann Kolbe (1818–1884) folgt 1865 dem Ruf auf einen Leipziger Lehrstuhl, wo er seine Forschungen in einem 1868 in der heutigen Liebigstraße eröffneten modernen Laboratorium verfolgt. 1887 übernimmt Wilhelm Ostwald eine Professur in Leipzig, die wissenschaftlich und industriell viele Früchte tragen soll. In der Medizinischen Fakultät entstehen unter dem Pharmakologen Rudolf Boehm (1844–1926) hochmoderne Laboratorien, ein Hörsaal mit 180 Plätzen und ein Mikroskopiersaal.

FIRST FEMALE DOCTOR

Another revolution took place at the University of Leipzig at the end of the century: In 1880 Hope Bridge Adams from England was the first woman to take the medical state examination at a German university, at a time when the enrolment of female applicants for a place at university was unthinkable. This might have been the reason why the Faculty of Medicine enabled her to take the state examination but refused her a doctorate. A few years earlier, the jurists had admitted a woman to examinations as well; and a Russian woman could take a doctorate in 1873.

The transformation of Saxony from an agrarian to an industrial economy in the last third of the 19th century became clearly visible in the strongly differentiating variety of subjects at the University of Leipzig. The chemist Hermann Kolbe (1818–1884) accepted an appointment to a Leipzig chair in 1865, where he carried out his research in a modern laboratory, which was opened in today's *Liebigstraße* in 1868. In 1887 Wilhelm Ostwald took up a professorship in Leipzig, which was to yield many results in science and industry. At the Faculty of Medicine, highly modern laboratories, a lecture hall with 180 seats and a microscopy hall were built under the pharmacologist Rudolf Boehm (1844–1926).

Das »Triersche Institut« 1892 in der Liebig-, Ecke Stephanstraße.
The "Triersche Institute" in Liebigstraße, *on the corner of* Stephanstraße.

Rechts: Kinderklinik im Ende des 19. Jahrhunderts neu entstehenden Medizinischen Viertel.
Right: Pediatric clinic in the newly emerging Medical Quarter at the end of the 19th century.

DAS 19. JAHRHUNDERT
THE 19TH CENTURY

BLICK IN DIE WELT
VIEW OF THE WORLD

1804 Der Code civil tritt als bürgerliches Gesetzbuch in Frankreich in Kraft und erobert Europa. The Napoleonic Code is enforced as code of civil law in France and conquers Europe.

1807 Die USA und England verbieten den Sklavenhandel. The U.S. and England ban the slave trade.

1815 Napoleon verliert die Schlacht von Waterloo und wird endgültig gestürzt. Napoleon loses the Battle of Waterloo and is finally overthrown.

1840 In Großbritannien erscheint mit dem One Penny Black die erste Briefmarke der Welt. In Great Britain, the One Penny Black is the first stamp to appear in the world.

1859 Charles Darwin begründet die moderne Evolutionstheorie. Charles Darwin establishes modern evolution theory.

1861 In den USA bricht der Bürgerkrieg zwischen Nord- und Südstaaten aus. Civil War breaks out between the Northern and the Southern States in the U.S.

1867 Karl Marx veröffentlicht den ersten Band seines Hauptwerks »Das Kapital«. Karl Marx publishes the first volume of his chief work "Das Kapital".

1869 Der Suezkanal schafft eine Verbindung zwischen Mittelmeer und Rotem Meer. The Suez Canal creates a link between the Mediterranean and the Red Sea.

1871 Otto von Bismarck wird erster Kanzler des vereinigten deutschen Kaiserreiches. Otto von Bismarck becomes the first Chancellor of the united German Empire.

1876 Die Sioux-Indianer erringen bei der Schlacht am Little Bighorn ihren letzten Sieg. The Sioux Indians gain their last victory in the Battle of the Little Bighorn.

1886 Carl Friedrich Benz lässt seinen benzinbetriebenen Motorwagen patentieren. Carl Friedrich Benz has his gasoline-powered motorcar patented.

1895 Die Brüder Auguste und Louis Lumière starten in Paris den Siegeszug des Kinofilms. The brothers Auguste and Louis Lumière start the triumph of the cinefilm in Paris.

1896 Pierre Baron de Coubertin organisiert die ersten Olympischen Spiele der Neuzeit in Athen. Pierre Baron de Coubertin organizes the first Olympic Games in modern history in Athens.

BERÜHMTHEITEN AN DER UNIVERSITÄT
ILLUSTRIOUS PEOPLE AT THE UNIVERSITY

Paul Flechsig 1847 – 1929
Hirnforscher und Mitbegründer der modernen Psychiatrie, ab 1865 Studium, 1875 Habilitation, ab 1882 Lehrstuhl für Psychiatrie, 1894/95 Rektor. Brain researcher and co-founder of modern psychiatry, from 1865 study, 1875 postdoctoral studies, from 1882 Chair of Psychiatry, 1894/95 Rector.

Robert Schumann 1810 – 1856
Komponist und Pianist der Romantik, 1828 Immatrikulation an der Juristenfakultät, 1840 Hochzeit mit Clara Wieck, 1843 Lehrer am Konservatorium. Composer and pianist of Romanticism, 1828 enrolment at the Faculty of Law, 1840 marriage to Clara Wieck, 1843 teacher at the conservatory.

Friedrich Ratzel 1844 – 1904
Begründer der Anthropogeographie und Politischen Geographie, 1886 Berufung auf Lehrstuhl für Geographie, zu seinen Vorlesungen drängen sich die Studenten. Founder of anthropogeography and political geography, 1886 appointment to the Chair of Geography; students crowded into his lectures.

Franz Mehring 1846 – 1919
Publizist, Politiker, Historiker, 1866 bis 1870 Studium der Philologie und Geschichte, 1882 Promotion, fünf Jahre Chefredakteur der Leipziger Volkszeitung. Journalist, politician, historian, 1866 to 1870 study of philology and history, 1882 doctorate, chief editor for five years at the daily *Leipziger Volkszeitung*.

Friedrich Nietzsche 1844 – 1900
Philosoph und Schriftsteller, ab 1865 Studium, 1869 Ernennung zum Doktor der Philosophie ohne Prüfung, ohne eingereichte Arbeit und in Abwesenheit. Philosopher and writer, from 1865 study, 1869 appointment to Doctor of Philosophy without examination, without handing in a dissertation and in absentee.

20.

ZWEI WELTKRIEGE, ZWEI DIKTATUREN UND EIN DEMOKRATISCHER NEUANFANG

TWO WORLD WARS, TWO DICTATORSHIPS AND A DEMOCRATIC NEW BEGINNING

Die Universität Leipzig nimmt zum Ende des 19. und Beginn des 20. Jahrhunderts eine Spitzenstellung nicht nur in Deutschland ein. Das lässt sich unter anderem an der großen Zahl von Nobelpreisträgern ablesen, die mit der Alma mater Lipsiensis verbunden sind. Theodor Mommsen, der 1848 als außerordentlicher Professor für Rechtswissenschaften an der Universität unterrichtete, ist der erste ehemalige Leipziger, der die hohe Auszeichnung erhält. 1902 wird ihm der Literatur-Nobelpreis als »dem gegenwärtig größten lebenden Meister der historischen Darstellungskunst, mit besonderer Berücksichtigung seines monumentalen Werkes ›Römische Geschichte‹« verliehen. Auch Wilhelm Ostwald, der im Jubiläumsjahr 1909 den Chemie-Nobelpreis »als Anerkennung für seine Arbeiten über die Katalyse sowie für seine grundlegenden Untersuchungen über chemische Gleichgewichtsverhältnisse und Reaktionsgeschwindigkeiten« bekommt, ist zu dieser Zeit nicht mehr an der Alma mater tätig.

Weltweit hohes Ansehen genießt Werner Heisenberg, der 1927 mit 26 Jahren als Professor an die Universität Leipzig kommt. 1932 erhält er den Physik-Nobelpreis. Auch Felix Bloch, der 1931 als Assistent bei Heisenberg arbeitet, bekommt 1952 den Preis in diesem Fach. 1965 dann der Japaner Sin-Itiro Tomonaga, der von 1937 bis 1939 einen Forschungsaufenhalt bei Heisenberg in Leipzig absolviert. Ab 1954 leitet Gustav Hertz, Nobelpreisträger von 1925, das Physikalische Institut. Weitere Preisträger mit Leipziger Hintergrund sind unter anderen Gustav Stresemann, der 1926 den Friedens-Nobelpreis erhält, und Carl Bosch, der 1898 in Leipzig promoviert und dem 1931 der Nobelpreis in Chemie verliehen wird.

The University of Leipzig held a top rank, and not only in Germany, at the end of the 19th and the beginning of the 20th century. This can be seen in the great number of Nobel Prize Laureates who were connected with the Alma mater Lipsiensis. Theodor Mommsen, who taught as associate professor of law at the University in 1848, was the first person from Leipzig to receive the distinct award. In 1902 he was awarded the Nobel Prize in Literature as "the greatest living master of the art of historical writing, with special reference to his monumental work, 'A history of Rome'". Also, Wilhelm Ostwald, who was no longer working at the Alma mater at that time, received the Nobel Prize in Chemistry in the anniversary year of 1909 "in recognition of his work on catalysis and for his investigations into the fundamental principles governing chemical equilibria and rates of reaction".

Werner Heisenberg, aged 26, came to the University of Leipzig in 1927 as a professor and enjoyed an excellent reputation worldwide. In 1932 he was awarded the Nobel Prize in Physics. Felix Bloch, who worked as an assistant with Heisenberg in 1931, also received the Nobel Prize in the same field. Likewise Sin-Itiro Tomonaga from Japan in 1965, who was a visiting researcher with Heisenberg in Leipzig from 1937 to 1939. From 1954 Gustav Hertz, Nobel Prize Laureate of 1925, led the Institute of Physics. Further Nobel Laureates who had a Leipzig background were, for instance, Gustav Stresemann, who received the Nobel Peace Prize in 1926, and Carl Bosch, who had completed his doctorate in Leipzig in 1898 and was awarded the Nobel Prize in Chemistry in 1931.

Symbolträchtig: Paulinerglocke und Nikolaikirche.
Deeply symbolic: Pauliner *Bell and St. Nicholas Church.*

Vorlesung im 1956 eröffneten Neubau des Instituts für Anatomie.
Lecture at the Institute of Anatomy in the new building opened in 1956.

STOLZE FEIER

Natürlich sind solche Auszeichnungen hart erarbeitet, kommt der Erfolg Leipziger Wissenschaftler nicht von ungefähr. Zur 500-Jahr-Feier 1909 kann die »Arbeitsuniversität« auf ihre Weltgeltung verweisen. Der damalige Oberbürgermeister der Stadt, Rudolf Dittrich, spricht von einem »ungeahnten Wachstum und Aufblühen«. Er unterstreicht, dass sich die Universität in der Stadt wohl fühle und dass Leipzig stolz sei auf seine Universität. »Beide erkennen und genießen dankbar die Förderung, die sie einander gewähren«, konstatiert der Kommunalpolitiker zum Jubiläum.

Die seinerzeit sozialdemokratische Leipziger Volkszeitung schreibt zum Jubiläum, dass »das reiche Lob, das heute in der gesamten bürgerlichen Presse gespendet wird, beweist, daß heute die Bourgeoisie mit der Universität zufrieden ist, daß sie die Aufgabe erfüllt, die ihr innerhalb der bürgerlichen Gesellschaft gestellt ist«.

Das Studium ist zu dieser Zeit längst keine Männerdomäne mehr. Nach heftigen Debatten verabschiedet das Königlich-Sächsische Ministerium für Kultus und öffentlichen Unterricht am 10. April 1906 den Erlass, dass sich vom Sommersemester an auch Frauen immatrikulieren dürfen. Seit 1870 konnten sie bereits als Gasthörerinnen an Vorlesungen teilnehmen.

Vorreiterin ist die Universität Leipzig bei der Einrichtung einer Studienberatung. Als zweite deutsche Hochschule nach der Königlichen Friedrich-Wilhelm-Universität zu Berlin eröffnet sie 1912 eine »Amtliche Akademische Auskunftsstelle«, später ist diese sogar für ganz Sachsen zuständig.

PROUD CELEBRATION

The Leipzig scientists worked arduously for these awards. They were successful for good reason. On the occasion of its 500th anniversary celebration, the "Work University" could take pride in its international standing. The then Lord Mayor of the city, Rudolf Dittrich, spoke about an "unforeseen growth and flourishing". He underscored that the University was a right fit for the city and that Leipzig was proud of its University. "Both recognize and gratefully enjoy their mutual support", the local politician stated at the jubilee.

The then social democratic daily *Leipziger Volkszeitung* wrote at the anniversary that, "the rich praise given throughout the civil press today proves that the bourgeoisie is satisfied with the University, which fulfills its task assigned within civil society".

Study was far from being male dominated by this time. The Royal Saxon Ministry for Culture and Public Education, after heated debates, passed an order on 10 April 1906, which stated women were allowed to enrol, beginning with the summer semester. They had been able to take part in lectures as auditors from 1870.

The University of Leipzig was a trailblazer in the establishment of a student advisory service. It was the second German university, after the Royal Friedrich Wilhelm University in Berlin, to open an "Official Academic Information Office", and later would be responsible for all of Saxony.

Rektor mit Dekanen im Jubiläumsjahr 1909 (von links): Rudolf Boehm (Medizin), Ludwig Ihmels (Theologie), Karl Binding (Rektor), Adolf Wach (Jura), Gerhard Seeliger (Philosophie).

Rector and Deans in the jubilee year 1909 (from left): Rudolf Boehm (Medicine), Ludwig Ihmels (Theology), Karl Binding (Rector), Adolf Wach (Law), Gerhard Seeliger (Philosophy).

***Links:* Der Paulinerhof zu Beginn des 20. Jahrhunderts.**
Left: The Paulinerhof at the beginning of the 20th century.

Festhalle zur 500-Jahr-Feier auf dem Messplatz am Frankfurter Tor.
Festive hall for the 500th anniversary celebration in the Messplatz square at Frankfurt Gate.

BLUTIGER KRIEG

Voll nationaler Begeisterung ziehen die Deutschen in den Krieg von 1914. Erst später wird man ihn als Weltkrieg bezeichnen. Der Blutzoll ist auch in Leipzig riesig: Fast 1 400 Gefallene hat allein die Universität zu beklagen, eine bedeutende Epoche der Hochschule findet zugleich ihr abruptes Ende.

Einer, der selbst in den Krieg zog und dies als Antimilitarist später immer wieder beschreibt, ist der Student Erich Kästner. Mit einem Stipendium der Stadt Dresden für sein ausgezeichnetes Abitur in der Tasche kommt er 1919 nach Leipzig und studiert Geschichte, Philosophie, Germanistik und Theatergeschichte. Doch die Inflation frisst seine spärlichen Mittel auf, das Stipendium reicht nicht mehr. Kästner nimmt verschiedene Tätigkeiten auf, verkauft unter anderem Parfüm, und finanziert sein Studium aus dem Geld, das er als Journalist und Theaterkritiker der Neuen Leipziger Zeitung verdient. 1925 promoviert er über Friedrich den Großen und die deutsche Literatur.

Die Inflation bedeutet auch empfindliche Rückschläge in der Wissenschaftsentwicklung und im Lehrbetrieb. Wissenschaftliche Zeitschriften und Publikationen stellen ihr Erscheinen ein, an den Fakultäten fehlt das Geld für Instrumente, für Versuche, für Chemikalien. Dienstreisen werden unbezahlbar. Um so wichtiger ist es für die Hochschule, dass sich 1920 die »Gesellschaft von Förderern und Freunden der Universität Leipzig« konstituiert, parallel zur »Notgemeinschaft der deutschen Wissenschaft«.

Trotz aller Probleme kommt das wissenschaftliche Leben nicht zum Stillstand. 1923 wird die Tierärztliche Hochschule Dresden als Veterinärmedizinische Fakultät in die Universität Leipzig integriert. Ein Jahr später öffnet das »Pädagogische Institut für Volksschullehrer«. 1925 bedeutet die Einrichtung des Ordinariats für Pädagogik und Leibesübungen, dass es erstmals in Deutschland eine Sportprofessur gibt. Innerhalb kürzester Zeit hat es die Universität geschafft, sich wieder einen Spitzenplatz zu erobern, Studenten aus dem In- und Ausland strömen nach Leipzig. Internationale Anerkennung genießen vor allem die Medizinische Fakultät und die Naturwissenschaften. Doch auch die Geisteswissenschaften haben mit Theodor Frings einen großen Gelehrten in ihren Reihen, 1927 folgt er dem Ruf nach Leipzig und wird Professor für Germanistik.

BLOODY WAR

Full of national enthusiasm, the Germans went off to the war of 1914. Only later would it be called World War. The death toll was enormous in Leipzig: the University alone mourned almost 1,400 soldiers killed in action. At the same time, an important era at the University came to an abrupt ending.

The student Erich Kästner went to war himself and later described this as antimilitarist again and again. He came to Leipzig in 1919 on a scholarship from the city of Dresden in his pocket, granted for his excellent A-levels. Kästner studied history, philosophy, the German language and literature and theatre history. But inflation ate up his sparse means, the scholarship was not sufficient any more. Kästner took up several jobs, such as selling perfume and financed his studies with the money he earned as a journalist and theatre critic with the paper *Neue Leipziger Zeitung*. In 1925 he completed his doctorate, with a thesis on Frederick the Great and German literature.

Denkmal mit 1 396 Namen der im Ersten Weltkrieg gefallenen Universitätsangehörigen.
Monument, with 1,396 names of University staff killed in action in World War One.

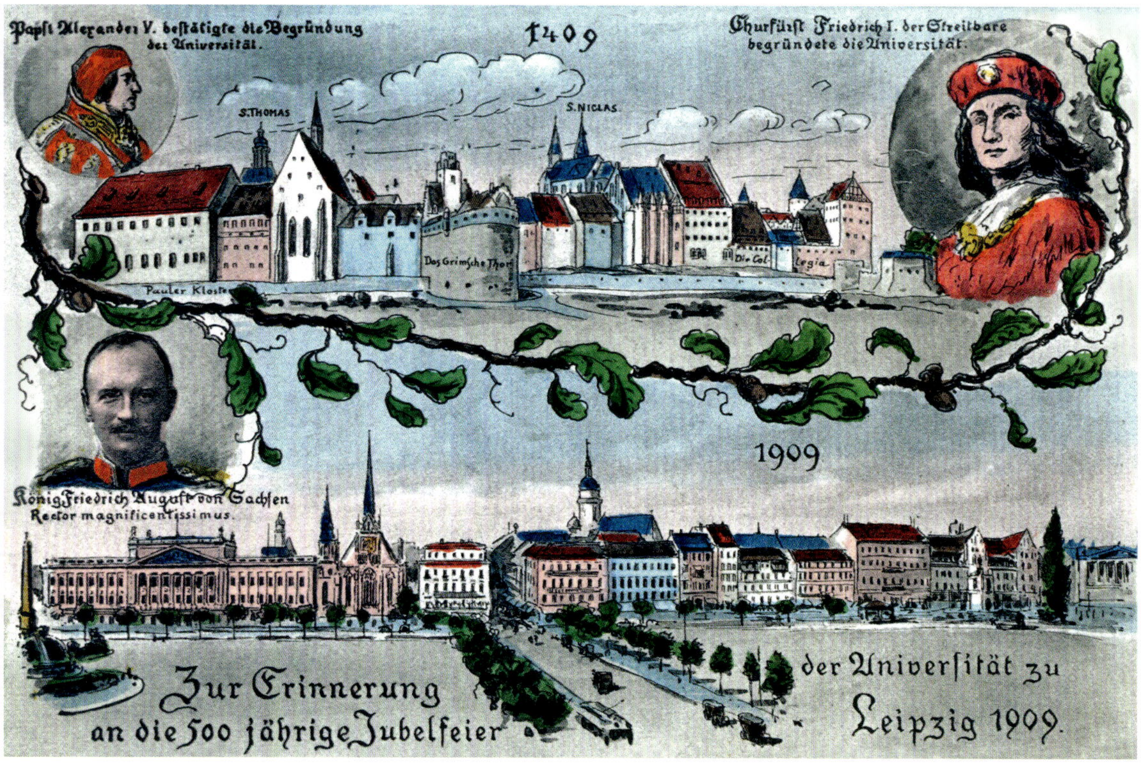

Postkarte mit Papst, Kurfürst und König zur Jubelfeier 1909.
Postcard showing Pope, Elector and King at the jubilee in 1909.

Sternwarte der Universität um 1912.
University observatory circa 1912.

DUNKLES KAPITEL

Nur wenige Jahre später beginnt eines der dunkelsten Kapitel in der Geschichte der Alma mater Lipsiensis. Schon 1931 gelingt es dem nationalsozialistischen Studentenbund, an der Universität Fuß zu fassen und im Allgemeinen Studentenausschuss die Mehrheit zu erringen. Auch unter den Professoren gibt es nicht wenige Anhänger von Adolf Hitlers NSDAP. Der Soziologe Hans Freyer spricht sich 1930 in seiner Schrift »Die Revolution von rechts« für eine Veränderung der bürgerlich-parlamentarischen Herrschaft aus, die er für überholt erachtet. Im März 1933 befürworten mehr als 100 Professoren in einem Aufruf die Wahl der Hitlerpartei in den Reichstag. Der Theologe, Kirchenhistoriker und Archäologe Hans Achelis, 1932/33 Rektor der Universität, begrüßt am 14. Mai 1933 die Bücherverbrennung der Nationalsozialisten, der unter anderem auch die Werke Erich Kästners zum Opfer fallen. Achelis euphorisch: »Wenn jetzt die Jugend den Kampf eröffnet gegen schlechte Literatur, so jauchzen wir der Jugend zu.« An der Leipziger Kinderklinik wird ab 1933 so genannter »erbkranker Nachwuchs« zwangssterilisiert und damit das »Rassehygiene-Programm« der Nazis unmittelbar umgesetzt.

Das »Reichsgesetz zur Wiederherstellung des Berufsbeamtentums« erlaubt es den nationalsozialistischen Machthabern nach dem 7. April 1933 politisch missliebige oder jüdische Beamte aus dem Dienst zu entfernen. Mehr als 30 Hochschullehrer werden von der Universität Leipzig vertrieben, unter anderem der Historiker Walter Goetz, der Landwirtschaftswissenschaftler Adolf Zade und der Jurist Erwin Jacobi, der nach Kriegsende jedoch zurückkehrt und zwischen

Inflation meant considerable setbacks in the academic development of science and teaching. Scientific journals and periodicals ceased publication, the faculties lacked money for instruments, experiments and chemical products. Travelling on university business became unaffordable. All the more important for the institution, the "Society of Friends and Patrons of the University of Leipzig" was instituted in 1920, parallel to the "Emergency Association of German Science".

Despite all problems, academic life did not come to a standstill. In 1923 the Dresden Veterinary College was integrated into the University of Leipzig as the Faculty of Veterinary Medicine. The "Pedagogical Institute for Elementary Teachers" opened one year later. The establishment of the Chair of Pedagogy and Physical Exercise in 1925 meant that there was a Chair of Sports for the first time in Germany. The University successfully recaptured a top rank within an incredibly short time. Students from Germany and abroad flocked to Leipzig. In particular the Faculty of Medicine and the natural sciences enjoyed an international reputation. Humanities included, with Theodor Frings, a great scholar among their ranks. He accepted the appointment to Leipzig and became professor of German studies in 1927.

DARK CHAPTER

One of the darkest chapters in the history of the Alma mater Lipsiensis was to begin only a few years later. The National Socialist Student Confederation successfully gained a foothold at the University and won the majority in the general students' executive committee

Links: Geschmücktes Portal des Augusteums.
Left: Decorated portal of the Augusteum.

Studentisches Festkomitee von 1909.
Student celebration committee of 1909.

1947 und 1949 als Rektor agiert. Der Mathematiker Friedrich Levi flieht 1935 vor den Nazis, der Mittelalter-Experte Siegmund Hellmann stirbt 1942 im Konzentrationslager Theresienstadt. Zudem erkennen die Nationalsozialisten zahlreichen jüdischen Absolventen der Universität die hier erworbenen Doktortitel ab.

SCHWERE VERLUSTE

Doch es gibt auch Widerstand gegen die Terrorherrschaft. Der Jurist Hermann Reinmuth wird 1934 verhaftet und wegen »Vorbereitung zum Hochverrat« zu sieben Jahren Zuchthaus verurteilt. 1941 soll er entlassen werden, weigert sich aber, die übliche Erklärung,

as early as 1931. Among professors, there were more than a few adherents to Adolf Hitler's National Socialist Party (NSDAP). The sociologist Hans Freyer, in his article *Die Revolution von rechts* ("The revolution from the right") in 1930, argued for a move away from civil parliamentary rule which he considered outdated. In March 1933, more than 100 professors, in an appeal, approved of the election of Hitler's party into the *Reichstag*. The theologian, church historian and archeologist Hans Achelis, 1932/33 Rector of the University, welcomed the book burning by the Nazis on 14 May 1933, to which, for instance, the works of Erich Kästner fell victim. Achelis stated euphorically: "When now youth begins the battle against bad

Fassritt-Szene aus Goethes »Faust« im Umzug zum 500. Gründungsjubiläum.
Barrel ride scene from Goethe's "Faust" in the procession at the 500th jubilee.

Die Physiker Werner Heisenberg (hinten) und Friedrich Hund (rechts) mit Studenten.
The physicists Werner Heisenberg (behind) and Friedrich Hund (right) with students.

Rechts: Gustav Hertz, von 1954 bis 1961 Direktor des Physikalischen Instituts.
Right: Gustav Hertz, Director of the Institute of Physics from 1954 to 1961.

Wolfgang Natonek, liberaler Studentenratsvorsitzender in den Jahren 1947/48.
Wolfgang Natonek, liberal chairman of student council in the years 1947/48.

in Zukunft nichts mehr gegen den NS-Staat zu unternehmen, zu unterschreiben. Er wird ins KZ Sachsenhausen eingeliefert, wo er am 27. April stirbt. Die Pädagogin Maria Grollmuß, die mit Reinmuth befreundet ist, unterstützt politische Gefangene, transportiert illegale Literatur und hilft Verfolgten bei der Flucht. Wie Reinmuth am 7. April 1934 verhaftet, wird sie in das berüchtigte Zuchthaus Waldheim gebracht, im Dezember 1940 kommt sie ins KZ Ravensbrück, am 6. August 1944 stirbt sie dort.

Nach dem intellektuellen Niedergang – die Studentenzahl sinkt von 7 224 im Wintersemester 1932/33 auf 1 002 im Jahr 1944 – erleidet die Universität nach Beginn des Zweiten Weltkriegs auch schwere materielle Verluste. In den Kriegsjahren 1943 bis 1945 fallen alliierte Bomben und verursachen extreme Schäden. Am Ende des Krieges sind von 103 Lehr- und Forschungseinrichtungen 67 vollständig zerstört. Nahezu 64 Prozent der Universität, ihrer Kliniken, das Gros ihrer geistes- und naturwissenschaftlichen Institute, Laboratorien, Sammlungen und Fachbibliotheken bestehen nicht mehr.

WECHSELNDE MACHTHABER

Am 18. April 1945 nehmen amerikanische Truppen Leipzig ein, am 8. Mai kapituliert Deutschland – der Krieg ist vorbei. Bereits am 16. Mai wird der

literature, we cheer to the youth." At the Leipzig pediatric clinic, from 1933 so-called "hereditarily-diseased offspring" was forced to be sterilized and thus, the "Racial hygiene" programme of the Nazis was immediately applied.

The "Law for the Restoration of the Professional Civil Service" enabled national socialist rulers to dismiss politically disliked and Jewish civil servants from office after 7 April 1933. More than 30 professors were expelled from the University of Leipzig such as the historian Walter Goetz, the agricultural scientist Adolf Zade and the jurist Erwin Jacobi, who returned after the end of the war and was Rector between 1947 and 1949. The mathematician Friedrich Levi fled the Nazis in 1935, the Middle Ages expert Siegmund Hellmann died in the Theresienstadt concentration camp in 1942. Furthermore the Nazis denied numerous Jewish graduates of the University the doctoral degrees they had obtained there.

HEAVY LOSSES

There was, however, resistance against the regime of terror as well. The jurist Hermann Reinmuth was arrested in 1934 and sentenced to seven years at a penitentiary for "preparing to commit high treason". In 1941 he was to be released but refused to sign the usual declaration specifying he would do nothing

Karikaturen der Germanisten August Korff und Theodor Frings.
Caricatures of the Germanists August Korff and Theodor Frings.

Rechts: Psychiatrie-Vorlesung Anfang des 20. Jahrhunderts.
Right: Psychiatry lecture at the beginning of the 20th century.

Operation in der Chirurgischen Poliklinik im Jahr 1915.
Operation in the surgical polyclinic in the year 1915.

Archäologie-Professor Bernhard Schweitzer neuer Rektor der Universität Leipzig. Als erste Amtshandlung wählt Schweitzer Dekane aus und ernennt am 19. Mai seinen Freund Hans-Georg Gadamer zum kommissarischen Dekan der Philosophischen Fakultät. Problematisch für den Neubeginn ist jedoch, dass die Amerikaner eine ganze Reihe von Wissenschaftlern – auch unter Androhungen durch den Geheimdienst CIC – zwingen, in den Westen zu gehen. Denn nach der Konferenz von Jalta ist klar, dass die Sowjetarmee in Leipzig einmarschieren wird.

Am 2. Juli 1945 nimmt die sowjetische Militäradministration wie vorgesehen ihren Platz ein. Die Besatzungsmacht trennt sich bald von Schweitzer, der als zu zögerlich gilt. Am 21. Januar 1946 wird Hans-Georg Gadamer zum neuen Rektor gewählt, der die geisteswissenschaftliche, humanistische und unabhängige Tradition der Hochschule verkörpert. Im Gegensatz

against the national socialist state in the future. He was then taken to the Sachsenhausen concentration camp, where he died on 27 April. The pedagogue Maria Grollmuß, who was friends with Reinmuth, supported political prisoners, transported illegal literature and assisted in the escape of those persecuted. Arrested on the same day as Reinmuth, on 7 April 1934, she was taken to the infamous Waldheim penitentiary. In December 1940 she was sent to the Ravensbrück concentration camp, where she died on 6 August 1944.

After the intellectual decline – the student numbers plummeted from 7,224 in the winter semester 1932/33 to 1,002 in 1944 – the University suffered heavy material losses after the beginning of the Second World War as well. Allied bombs fell in the war years 1943 to 1945 and caused extreme damages. 67 of the 103 teaching and research facilities were completely

Links: Medizinball-Reparatur im 1925 gegründeten Institut für Leibesübungen.
Left: Repair of medicine balls at the Institute of Physical Education, founded in 1925.

Wehrmachtsausstellung 1943 auf dem Augustusplatz.
Wehrmacht *exhibition at the* Augustusplatz *square in 1943.*

Leibniz-Denkmal und Universität am Ende des Zweiten Weltkriegs.
Leibniz monument and the University at the end of the Second World War.

zu Schweitzer lässt Gadamer auch Marxisten für den Lehrkörper zu, sofern sie als qualifiziert gelten. Bei der Wiedereröffnung der Universität am 5. Februar 1946 zählen 101 Personen zum Lehrpersonal, während es zuletzt im Krieg 340 waren.

NEUE FAKULTÄT

Charakteristisch für die ersten Jahre nach dem Zweiten Weltkrieg an der Universität sind die konsequente Entnazifizierung, das Wirken humanistisch gesinnter bürgerlicher Wissenschaftler im Geiste des demokratischen Neuanfangs und die sukzessive Ausbreitung marxistischer Ideen unter den Wissenschaftlern und Studenten.

destroyed after the war. Almost 64 percent of the University, its clinics, and the greater part of its institutes of humanities and natural sciences, laboratories, collections and specialized libraries no longer existed.

CHANGING RULERS

American troops took over Leipzig on 18 April 1945 and Germany surrendered on 8 May. The war was over. As early as on 16 May, the professor of archeology Bernhard Schweitzer became new Rector of the University of Leipzig. Schweitzer, in a first official act, selected the Deans and appointed his friend Hans-Georg Gadamer temporary Dean of the Faculty of

Studenten und Lehrkräfte beim Arbeitseinsatz in Kriegstrümmern.
Students and teaching staff on work duty in the war rubble.

Rechts: Feierliche Wiedereröffnung der Universität am 5. Februar 1946.
Right: Festive reopening of the University on 5 February 1946.

Links: Rede von Rektor Georg Mayer am 11. Juni 1954 in den Trümmern des Physikalischen Instituts.
Left: Speech of Rector Georg Mayer at the ruins of the Institute of Physics on 11 June 1954.

Ein deutliches Zeichen ist am 1. März die Einrichtung einer Vorstudienanstalt. Hier sollen sich solche Bewerber auf ein Studium vorbereiten, die wegen des Krieges, als Flüchtlinge oder Vertriebene, wegen politischer Verfolgung oder sozialer Benachteiligung kein Abitur ablegen konnten. 225 Arbeiter- und Bauernkinder zwischen 17 und 37 Jahren nehmen ein Studium im ersten Kurs auf. Ende 1947 wird die Vorstudienanstalt in die Universität eingegliedert. 1949 gehen aus den Anstalten, die es auch andernorts gibt, die Arbeiter-und-Bauern-Fakultäten (ABF) als gleichberechtigte Fakultäten an den Universitäten und Hochschulen hervor. In Leipzig nimmt die ABF am 1. Oktober 1949 mit 440 Studenten den Lehrbetrieb auf, erste Direktorin ist die Pädagogin Rosemarie Sacke-Gaudig.

In der ABF wird die Hochschulreife erworben. Den normalen Abiturstoff in den Fächern Deutsch, Geschichte, Gegenwartskunde, Geographie, Chemie, Physik, Mathematik, Russisch und Englisch oder Latein müssen die ABF-Studenten innerhalb von drei Jahren absolvieren. Nach dem ersten Studienjahr spezialisiert sich die Ausbildung in gesellschaftswissenschaftliche,

Philosophy on 19 May. The new beginning of the University was overshadowed by the Americans forcing a number of scientists to go to the West, some of them received menacing threats from the CIC secret service. For after the Yalta Conference, it was evident that the Soviet army would march into Leipzig.

On 2 July 1945 the Soviet military administration took up its position as scheduled. The occupying power soon parted with Schweitzer who was considered too hesitant. On 21 January 1946 Hans-Georg Gadamer was elected to be the new Rector. He embodied the arts-oriented, humanist and independent tradition of academia. Unlike Schweitzer, Gadamer admitted marxists onto the teaching staff as well, provided they were considered qualified. Upon the reopening of the University on 5 February 1946, the teaching staff numbered 101 people, while there were 340 during the war.

NEW FACULTY

Consequent denazification, the work of humanistic civil scientists in the spirit of the democratic renewal and the gradual spread of marxist ideas among scientists and students, were characteristic of the first years after the Second World War at the University. The setup of a pre-study institution, on 1 March, was a clear signal: applicants who were not able to qualify for university entrance due to the war prepared for university study. These applicants, who took up a course of study in the first session, included refugees or displaced people, and people who were politically persecuted or socially disadvantaged – 225 working-class and peasants' children, aged between 17 and 37. The pre-study institution was integrated into the University at the end of 1947. In 1949 the *Arbeiter-und-Bauern-Fakultäten (ABF)* (Workers and Peasants Faculties) emerged as equal faculties at the universities and other institutions of higher education, from the facilities which existed also in other places. The *ABF* in Leipzig began its teaching activities with 440 students on 1 October 1949, and its first director was the pedagogue Rosemarie Sacke-Gaudig.

At the *ABF* the general qualification for university entrance could be obtained. ABF students had to

Philosoph Hans-Georg Gadamer, Rektor nach der Wiedereröffnung 1946.
Philosopher Hans-Georg Gadamer, Rector after the reopening in 1946.

Links: Das Augusteum 1953 mit Bildern von Marx, Engels, Lenin und Stalin.
Left: The Augusteum, with pictures of Marx, Engels, Lenin and Stalin in 1953.

Festveranstaltung zur Umbenennung in Karl-Marx-Universität 1953.
Festive event for the naming of Karl Marx University in 1953.

Sprengung der Universitätskirche am 30. Mai 1968 um 10 Uhr.
Blowup of the University Church on 30 May 1968 at 10 a.m.

Die Paulinerkirche vor und nach der Sprengung.
The Pauliner *Church before and after the blowup.*

mathematisch-naturwissenschaftliche und medizinisch-biologische Fachrichtungen. In die ABF aufgenommen werden – wie die Bezeichnung verrät – vor allem Arbeiter und Bauern, aber auch Opfer des Faschismus und deren Kinder. Stipendien, kostenloses und lebensmittelmarkenfreies Mittagessen sowie unentgeltliche Lehr- und Lernmittel schaffen die materielle Grundlage für ein Studium an der ABF.

Von Anfang an als Einrichtung auf Zeit vorgesehen, verliert die ABF Ende der 1950er-Jahre ihre Funktion, weil die Jugendlichen jetzt an den Erweiterten Oberschulen oder durch eine Berufsausbildung mit Abitur die Hochschulreife erreichen können. Die Leipziger ABF wird 1962 geschlossen, 5 000 Studenten haben sie absolviert.

master the normal content of this qualification in the required subjects: German, history, geography, chemistry, physics, mathematics, Russian and English or Latin within three years. After the first year, the students would specialize in either the social sciences, mathematics and natural sciences or medical-biological branches of study. Mainly workers and peasants were accepted to the *ABF* – as the name suggests – but also victims of fascism and their children. Grants, free, unrationed lunch as well as cost free teaching and learning aids provided the material foundation for study at the *ABF*.

Originally planned as a temporary institution, the *ABF* became redundant at the end of the 1950s

1998 errichtete Installation zur Erinnerung an die Paulinerkirche.
Installation erected in 1998 to commemorate the Pauliner *Church.*

MARXISTISCHES BEKENNTNIS

Das augenscheinlichste Bekenntnis zur Lehre des Marxismus-Leninismus wird mit der Umbenennung der Universität Leipzig in Karl-Marx-Universität vollzogen. Am 5. Mai 1953 erklärt Rektor Georg Mayer: »Von heute an wird nun eine der ältesten und ruhmreichsten deutschen Universitäten seinen Namen tragen und ich bin optimistisch genug zu hoffen, daß in Bälde Marxens gewaltiges Denkerhaupt vom Giebelfeld der neu erbauten Leipziger Universität sinnend und lächelnd zugleich auf das Gewühl des nach ihm benannten Platzes blicken wird.« Eine Prophezeiung, die sich erfüllt.

Trotz aller Ideologie vergessen die Leipziger Hochschullehrer nicht ihren Witz. Der Mathematikprofessor Walter Schnee stellt 1953 diese Aufgabe in einer Klausurarbeit: »Herr Schlau ladet zur Feier seines bestandenen Staatsexamens seine Kommilitonen und Kommilitoninnen ein und beschließt, folgendes einzukaufen: erstens Bier, die Flasche zu 50 Pfennig, zweitens süßen Most für die Studentinnen, die Flasche zu 3 Mark, drittens hochprozentigen Kognak, die Flasche zu 5 Mark, im ganzen 100 Flaschen zu 100 Mark. Er übersieht sofort, daß er, wenn er von jeder Sorte wenigstens eine Flasche besorgt, nur zwei Möglichkeiten hat, nämlich entweder die Studentinnen zu beglücken oder eine kräftige Sauferei zu veranstalten. Welches sind diese beiden Möglichkeiten?«

Universitätsbaustelle Anfang der 1970er-Jahre.
University building site at the beginning of the 1970s.

Aufstellung zur Maidemonstration 1951 und 1982.
Gathering for the Mayday demonstration in 1951 and 1982.

BARBARISCHER AKT

»Das Ding muss weg«, verlangt Staats- und Parteichef Walter Ulbricht 1968. Er meint die Universitätskirche St. Pauli, die ihm ein Dorn im Auge ist. Der Augustusplatz heißt inzwischen Karl-Marx-Platz – und die sozialistische Universität soll einen neuen Campus erhalten. Am 30. Mai 1968 lässt die Führung der Sozialistischen Einheitspartei Deutschlands (SED) die Universitätskirche St. Pauli sprengen, nachdem sie zuvor die nötigen Beschlüsse der Leipziger Stadtverordnetenversammlung und universitärer Gremien veranlasst hatte. Damit ist der letzte noch aus dem Mittelalter stammende und vollkommen intakte Traditionsbau der Universität vernichtet. Wenig später fällt das nur leicht kriegsbeschädigte Augusteum, das Hauptgebäude der Alma mater, derselben barbarischen Aktion zum Opfer.

as young people were now able to obtain the entrance qualification for higher education either at an *Erweiterte Oberschule* (extended secondary school) or in a vocational training programme including A-levels. 5,000 students had completed the course of study by the time the Leipzig *ABF* was closed in 1962.

COMMITMENT TO MARXISM

The University made its most evident commitment to the teachings of marxism-leninism when it was renamed to Karl Marx University. Rector Georg Mayer declared on 5 May 1953: "From today one of the oldest and most famous German universities will carry his name and I am optimistic enough to hope that soon enough Marx's giant thinker's head will look both contemplatively and smilingly, from the tympanum of the newly built Leipzig University, upon the melee in the square named after him." And it was a prophecy that would be accomplished.

Despite all ideology, the Leipzig professors did not forget their humour. The professor of mathematics Walter Schnee assigned the following task in a test in 1953: "Mr Smart invites his male and female fellow students to celebrate his successful state examination

Innenhof des 1973 übergebenen Universitätskomplexes am Augustusplatz.
Inner court of the University complex at Augustusplatz square, dedicated in 1973.

Rechts: Revolutionsnummer der 1966 als Studentenkabarett gegründeten »academixer«.
Right: Revolution scene of the "academixer", founded as a students' political cabaret in 1966.

Links: Blick in die 1973 eröffnete Zentralmensa.
Left: View into the central cafeteria, opened in 1973.

Studentenzimmer 1975 in Lößniger Wohnheim-Neubau.
Student room in the newly built residence hall in Lößnig *in 1975.*

Zwischen 1972 und 1978 entsteht zwischen dem heutigen Augustusplatz und der Universitätsstraße eine neues Gebäudeensemble. Zug um Zug werden das neue Hauptgebäude, das Universitätshochhaus, im Volksmund »Weisheitszahn« genannt, das Hörsaal- und Seminargebäude, der Mensatrakt und die Zweigstelle der Universitätsbibliothek übergeben. Am Hauptgebäude hängt eine 33 Tonnen schwere, 14 Meter breite und etwa sechs Meter hohe Bronze-Plastik mit Karl Marx im Zentrum. Die Vorahnung von Rektor Mayer hat sich erfüllt. Unterdessen gibt es auch die traditionellen Universitätsstrukturen nicht mehr: Nach der dritten Hochschulreform ersetzen ab 1968 Sektionen und Bereiche die Fakultäten.

GRÖSSTER STUDENTENKLUB

Mitte der 1970er-Jahre kommen Studenten auf die Idee, einen Teil der alten Stadtbefestigung auszugraben: die Moritzbastei. Einst Teil der städtischen Wehranlagen, stand nach deren Zerstörung die erste konfessionslose Bürgerschule Deutschlands auf ihren Grundmauern. Nach dem Zweiten Weltkrieg füllen nur noch Schutt und Baureste die Gewölbe. Ab 1974 graben insgesamt rund 30 000 Studenten, darunter auch die spätere Bundeskanzlerin Angela Merkel,

and decides to buy the following: first, beer at 50 *Pfennig* per bottle; second, sweet must for the female students at 3 *Mark* per bottle; third, high-proof cognac at 5 *Mark* per bottle – altogether 100 bottles at the price of 100 *Mark*. He realizes at once that when he buys at least one bottle of each, he has only two alternatives, these are either to please only the female students or to stage a heavy booze event. Which are those two alternatives?"

ACT OF BARBARISM

"That thing has to go", the Head of State and Party, Walter Ulbricht, insisted in 1968. He was referring to the University Church St. Pauli, which was a thorn in his side. The *Augustusplatz* square was meanwhile called *Karl-Marx-Platz* – and the socialist University was to be given a new campus. On 30 May 1968, the leaders of the Socialist Unity Party of Germany had the University Church St. Pauli blown up, after having arranged for the required decisions of the Leipzig City Council Assembly and University committees. In so doing, the last traditional building of the University, originating from the Middle Ages and completely intact, was wiped out. The Augusteum, the main building of the Alma mater, which had been only slightly

Das Bettenhaus in der Liebigstraße, einziger Klinikneubau der Universität in der DDR-Zeit.
Bettenhaus *(Recovery building) in* Liebigstraße, *only new clinic building at the University during the GDR period.*

Freilegung der Moritzbastei in den 1970er-Jahren – ab 1982 größter Studentenklub Europas.
Unearthing of the Moritzbastei *in the 1970s, from 1982 largest student club in Europe.*

Augustusplatz mit Bildermuseum und Universitätsgebäuden um 1925, als Karl-Marx-Platz mit Neuem Gewandhaus um 1985 (rechts) und wieder als Augustusplatz um die Jahrtausendwende (unten).
Augustusplatz *square with Fine Art Museum and University buildings circa 1925; as* Karl-Marx-Platz *with New* Gewandhaus *ca. 1985 (right) and, again, as* Augustusplatz *ca. at the turn of millenium (below).*

damals Physikstudentin an der Leipziger Universität, in gut 150 000 unbezahlten Arbeitsstunden die Moritzbastei wieder aus. 1979 öffnet der Oberkeller, 1982 schließlich der gesamte Komplex – und damit Europas größter Studentenklub.

POLITISCHE DOMINANZ

Zwar gibt es – so etwa im Jahr 1972 am Institut für Medizinische Mikrobiologie und Epidemiologie – auch eine Reihe von internationalen Tagungen, in deren Mittelpunkt naturwissenschaftliche Fragestellungen stehen. Doch immer mehr übernimmt die Politik die Führungsrolle und instrumentalisiert die Wissenschaft für sich. Symposien mit Titeln wie »Die Bedeutung des systematischen Studiums der Grundlagen des Marxismus-Leninismus für die Herausbildung und Festigung sozialistischer Grundüberzeugungen der Studierenden« lassen erahnen, in welche Richtung die Reise geht.

Fast 60 Jahre muss sich die Universität Leipzig den wechselnden Diktaturen unterwerfen, die immer wieder in ihre akademische Selbstverwaltung eingreifen. An

Lange Amtszeit: Historiker Lothar Rathmann, Rektor von 1975 bis 1987.
Long in office: historian Lothar Rathmann, Rector from 1975 to 1987.

damaged during the war, fell victim to the same barbaric action a little later.

A new ensemble of buildings emerged between today's *Augustusplatz* and *Universitätsstraße* from 1972 to 1978. Step by step, the new main building, the University high rise, called "wisdom tooth" in the vernacular, the lecture hall and seminar buildings, the cafeteria wing and the branch of the University library were inaugurated. A bronze plaque, with Karl Marx in its centre, measuring 14 meters across, six meters high and weighing 33 tons, was suspended from the main building. The prophecy of Rector Mayer had materialized. Meanwhile the traditional university structures had ceased to exist: sections and areas replaced the faculties after the third higher education reform in 1968.

LARGEST STUDENT CLUB

In the mid-1970s, students had the idea to excavate a part of the old city fortification: the *Moritzbastei*, formerly a part of the city's defence structures. After its destruction, Germany's first undenominational

Druckgrafiken von Siegfried Ratzlaff zum Universitätsjubiläum 1984 mit Darstellung der Paulinerkirche.
Graphic prints by Siegfried Ratzlaff depicting the Pauliner *Church for the University anniversary in 1984.*

die Opfer der beiden Zwangsherrschaften des 20. Jahrhunderts erinnern eine in der Bibliotheca Albertina angebrachte Ehrentafel und ein dort einsehbares Ehrenbuch. Mehr als 100 Namen umfasst die Liste der zwischen 1933 und 1989 verhafteten und eingesperrten Angehörigen der Universität, 16 Menschen werden benannt, die in der Haft gestorben sind oder hingerichtet wurden. Eines der letzten Todesurteile trifft den Studenten der Wirtschaftswissenschaften Herbert Belter – als Kopf einer Oppositionsgruppe 1950 verhaftet, am 20. Januar 1951 verurteilt und am 28. April 1951 in der Sowjetunion erschossen.

FRIEDLICHE REVOLUTION

Erst der politische Umbruch im Herbst 1989 und die Wiedervereinigung des seit vier Jahrzehnten geteilten Deutschlands im Jahr darauf ermöglicht die Erneuerung der Alma mater Lipsiensis. Zum ersten Mal seit 1933 wählt das Konzil im Februar 1991 in geheimer

secondary school stood on its foundations. Only rubble and debris filled the vaults after the Second World War. Starting from 1974, a total of about 30,000 students excavated the *Moritzbastei* in more than 150,000 unpaid man hours, among them the later to be Federal Chancellor Angela Merkel, at the time student of physics at the Leipzig University. In 1979 the upper cellar opened and in 1982, finally, the whole complex – and thus Europe's largest student club.

POLITICAL DOMINANCE

It is true that there was a series of international conferences focussing on questions of natural sciences, such as that held at the Institute of Medical Microbiology and Epidemiology in 1972. But increasingly, politics took the lead and exploited science for its purposes. Symposia entitled such as "The significance of systematic study of the foundations

Aufkleber vom Ferienlager auf der Insel Rügen 1989.
Sticker from a holiday camp on Rügen *island 1989.*

Links: Sozialistische Visionen im Stadtmodell von 1977.
Left: Socialist visions depicted in the city model of 1977.

Telefonzentrale der Universität 1984.
Telephone switchboard of the University in 1984.

Einsatz der Bereitschaftspolizei am 7. Oktober 1989, dem 40. und letzten Jahrestag der DDR.
Riot police in action on 7 October 1989, the 40th and last anniversary of the GDR.

Wahl den Rektor. Zugleich wird die Rückkehr zum alten Namen beschlossen und damit die Abkehr von der sozialistischen Programmatik auch nach außen verdeutlicht. Schmerzliche Einschnitte folgen: Die Zahl der Mitarbeiter muss von 14 000 auf rund 6 800 sinken. Disziplinen, die als besonders politisch belastet gelten, sollen abgewickelt oder in eine neue Richtung geführt werden. Erster demokratisch gewählter Rektor nach

of marxism-leninism for the emergence and consolidation of basic socialist beliefs of the students", for instance, indicated what path the University would take.

The University of Leipzig had to submit to alternating dictatorships, which would interfere with its academic self-government. Both a plaque of honour in the Bibliotheca Albertina and a book of honour which can be inspected there commemorate the victims of the two 20th century dictatorships. The list of people who were executed or died in prison comprises 16 names; and those who were arrested and imprisoned between 1933 and 1989 number 100. One of the last death sentences fell on Herbert Belter, a student of economics, who was arrested as the head of a small opposition group in 1950. He was convicted on 20 January 1951 and executed in the Soviet Union on 28 April 1951.

PEACEFUL REVOLUTION

Only political change in autumn 1989 and the reunification of Germany, which had been divided for four decades, one year later enabled the renewal of the Alma mater Lipsiensis. In a secret ballot for the first time since 1933, the *Konzil* (Council) elected the Rector in February 1991 and simultaneously decided to return to the University's old name. Thus the abandonment of the socialist programme was made evident externally. Severe cutbacks followed: The number of staff sank from 14,000 to approximately 6,800. Disciplines which were considered to be particularly politically charged, were to be phased out or led in a new direction. In 1991, the chemist Cornelius Weiss became the first democratically elected Rector

Montagsdemonstration am 9. Oktober 1989 auf dem Karl-Marx-Platz vor der Universität.
Monday demonstration on 9 October 1989, at Karl-Marx-Platz, *in front of the University.*

Aufbruch in eine neue Zeit: Kerzen zur alljährlichen Erinnerung an die friedliche Revolution vom Herbst 1989.
Departure into a new era: Candles annually commemorate the peaceful revolution of autumn 1989.

Rektor Horst Hennig bei der Gründung des Studentenrates am 9. November 1989.
Rector Horst Henning at the founding of the students' council on 9 November 1989.

Rechts: Cornelius Weiss, Rektor von 1991 bis 1997, und sein Nachfolger Volker Bigl (links), Magnifizenz bis 2003.
Right: Cornelius Weiss, Rector from 1991 to 1997, and his successor Volker Bigl (left), Rector until 2003.

der friedlichen Revolution wird 1991 der Chemiker Cornelius Weiss, der das Amt bis 1997 inne hat. Ihm folgt der Hirnforscher Volker Bigl, der wie Weiss der Universität seit Jahren aufs engste verbunden ist.

Die beiden Rektoren packen die schwere Aufgabe an, die geistig-moralische, personelle und strukturelle Erneuerung der Universität umzusetzen. Zudem sorgen sie für die Integration von Wissenschaftlern, die durch Neuberufungen – davon ein Drittel aus den alten Bundesländern – oder durch Zusammenschluss mit anderen Leipziger Hochschulen an die Universität gekommen sind. Die Bemühungen um eine moderne, weltoffene und zukunftsorientierte Alma mater sollen rasch vorankommen. Die am 8. Juni 1994 vom Konzil nach ausgiebiger Diskussion verabschiedete Verfassung bildet dafür die Grundlage. Die Universität geht frei ins neue Jahrtausend.

after the peaceful revolution. He held office until 1997, followed by the brain researcher Volker Bigl who, like Weiss, had been very closely connected to the University for years.

Both Rectors embraced the difficult task of implementing an intellectual-moral, personnel and structural renewal of the University. Furthermore, they provided for the integration of new academic staff who came to the University through new appointments – one-third of which came from the West German federal states – or through a merger with other Leipzig higher education institutions. The efforts towards a modern, cosmopolitan and future-oriented Alma mater were to advance quickly. The constitution passed by the *Konzil* after thorough discussion on 8 June 1994, laid the groundwork. The University moved freely into the new millenium.

Kroch-Haus, Universitätshauptgebäude und City-Hochhaus am Ende des 20. Jahrhunderts.
Kroch building, University main building and City highrise at the end of the 20th century.

DAS 20. JAHRHUNDERT
THE 20TH CENTURY

BLICK IN DIE WELT
VIEW OF THE WORLD

1901 In Stockholm und Oslo werden erstmals die Nobelpreise vergeben. In Stockholm and Oslo, the Nobel Prizes are awarded for the first time.

1903 Den Gebrüdern Wright gelingt der erste Motorflug. The Wright brothers manage to make the first engine powered flight.

1907 Finnland führt als erstes Land Europas das Frauenwahlrecht ein. Finland is the first European country to introduce womens' suffrage.

1912 Die Titanic versinkt nach der Kollision mit einem Eisberg. The Titanic sinks after colliding with an iceberg.

1914 Die Ermordung des österreichischen Thronfolgers in Sarajevo löst den Ersten Weltkrieg aus. The assassination of the Austrian heir to the throne in Sarajevo triggers the First World War.

1917 Die Oktoberrevolution bringt in Russland die Bolschewisten an die Macht. The October Revolution brings the Bolsheviks into power in Russia.

1929 Der Zusammenbruch des US-Aktienmarktes führt zur weltweiten Wirtschaftskrise. The crash of the U.S. stock market leads to worldwide economic crisis.

1937 Der größte jemals gebaut Zeppelin »Hindenburg« explodiert nach einem Transatlantikflug. The biggest ever built zeppelin “Hindenburg” explodes after a transatlantic flight.

1945 Der Zweite Weltkrieg geht mit der bedingungslosen Kapitulation Deutschlands zu Ende. The Second World War comes to an end with the unconditional surrender of Germany.

1961 Juri Gagarin fliegt als erster Mensch ins Weltall. Juri Gagarin is the first man to fly into space.

1965 Bob Dylan schreibt das zum besten Rocksong aller Zeiten gekürte »Like a Rolling Stone«. Bob Dylan writes “Like a Rolling Stone” to be named the best rock song of all times.

1989 Mit dem Zusammenbruch der Ostblock-Staaten fällt der Eiserne Vorhang in Europa. The Iron Curtain falls with the collapse of the Eastern Bloc States.

1994 Der Eurotunnel unter dem Ärmelkanal verbindet England und Frankreich. The Euro Tunnel under the English Channel links England and France.

BERÜHMTHEITEN AN DER UNIVERSITÄT
ILLUSTRIOUS PEOPLE AT THE UNIVERSITY

Hans Mayer 1907 – 2001
Literaturwissenschaftler und Jurist, 1948 bis 1963 Inhaber des Lehrstuhls für Literaturwissenschaft, 1992 Ehrendoktor, 2001 Ehrenbürger der Stadt Leipzig. Literary scholar and jurist, 1948 to 1963 holder of the Chair of Literary studies, 1992 honorary doctorate, 2001 honorary citizen of Leipzig.

Erich Kästner 1899 – 1974
Schriftsteller, ab 1919 Studium der Geschichte, Philosophie, Germanistik und Theaterwissenschaft, 1925 Promotion, bis 1927 Redakteur bei der Neuen Leipziger Zeitung. Writer, from 1919 study of history, philosophy, German studies and theatre studies,1925 doctorate, editor at the daily *Neue Leipziger Zeitung* until 1927.

Georg Steindorff 1861 – 1951
Ägyptologe, ab 1893 Inhaber des Lehrstuhls für Ägyptologie, bis 1939 Ausbau der kleinen Lehrsammlung zum Ägyptischen Museum der Universität. Egyptologist, from 1893 holder of the Chair of Egyptology, extension of the small teaching collection to the Egyptian Museum of the University until 1939.

Ernst Bloch 1885 – 1977
Philosoph, Begründer des »Prinzip Hoffnung«, 1948 Berufung auf Lehrstuhl für Philosophie, 1957 Zwangsemeritierung, ab 1961 Professor in Tübingen. Philosopher, founder of the “Principle of Hope”, 1948 appointment to the Chair of Philosophy, 1957 forced retirement and professor emeritus, from 1961 professor in Tübingen.

Carl Friedrich von Weizsäcker 1912 – 2007
Physiker, Philosoph, Friedensforscher, ab 1929 Physik- und Mathematikstudium, 1933 Promotion bei Werner Heisenberg, 1987 Ehrendoktor. Physicist, philosopher, peace researcher, from 1929 studies of physics and mathematics, 1933 PhD as a student of Werner Heisenberg, 1987 honorary doctorate.

21.

Die Universität im 21. Jahrhundert The University in the 21th Century

STUDENTENBOOM, FORSCHUNGSERFOLGE UND EIN NEUER CAMPUS ZUM JUBILÄUM
STUDENT BOOM, RESEARCH SUCCESS AND A NEW CAMPUS FOR THE ANNIVERSARY

Zu Beginn des 21. Jahrhunderts erlebt die Universität Leipzig einen in ihrer fast sechs Jahrhunderte langen Geschichte nie dagewesenen Zuspruch. Im Studienjahr 2004/05 sind an der Alma mater fast 31 000 Studenten eingeschrieben, darunter 5 600 Neuimmatrikulierte. Eigentlich ein freudiges Ergebnis, doch die Stellenzahl von Professoren und wissenschaftlichen Mitarbeitern wächst nicht mit, und die angespannte Finanzlage lässt der Universitätsleitung kaum Spielraum. Es soll gespart, gleichzeitig aber Forschung, Lehre und Studium verbessert werden. Gerade moderne Unterrichtsmethoden sind in den zu kleinen Seminarräumen und in die Jahre gekommenen Hörsälen am Campus Augustusplatz schwer umsetzbar. Der 29 Stockwerke hohe Uni-Riese, lange Zeit weit sichtbares Wahrzeichen der Alma mater, hat ausgedient und wird verkauft. Improvisation ist gefragt.

Alle Hoffnungen ruhen auf dem seit Jahren geplanten Neubau. Doch wo soll dieser entstehen und wie soll er aussehen? Jenseits der Innenstadt mit großflächiger Architektur und Infrastruktur nach amerikanischem Vorbild, oder im Herzen Leipzigs, wo die Universität seit ihrer Gründung 1409 beheimatet ist? Rasch wird klar: Sechs Jahrhunderte Universität bedeuten auch sechs Jahrhunderte Universitätsstadt. Leipzigs geistiges Zentrum gehört an den Augustusplatz, die Studenten prägen das Stadtbild. Doch lässt sich an der Stelle der 1968 gesprengten Universitätskirche St. Pauli ein Funktionsbau errichten? Die Diskussion erhitzt die Gemüter. Die Vorschläge reichen von der Rekonstruktion, wie ihn die Dresdner Frauenkirche erlebte, bis zu kühnen Plänen deutscher und ausländischer Stararchitekten. Auch die Leipziger Bürger mischen sich beherzt in den Diskurs ein, denn die Wunde der Kirchensprengung klafft noch immer.

At the beginning of the 21st century, the University of Leipzig experienced a popularity never before seen in its almost 600 years of history. Approximately 31,000 students were enrolled at the Alma mater in the academic year 2004/2005, among them 5,600 newly enrolled students. This is actually a good result, but the number of professors and academic staff did not grow accordingly and the tight financial situation did not give much scope to the University management: they had to save money, but at the same time, improve research, teaching and study. In particular, modern teaching methods were difficult to implement in the extremely small seminar rooms and the outdated lecture halls in the *Augustusplatz* campus. The 29 storey University highrise was now obsolete and subsequently sold. Improvisation was required.

All hopes were now pinned on the new building, which had been years in the planning. The question was where should it be built and what should it look like? Away from the inner city, with large-scale architecture and infrastructure according to the American model, or in the heart of Leipzig, where the University had been since its foundation in 1409? Soon it became obvious: six centuries of University also meant six centuries of a university city. The intellectual centre of Leipzig belonged to the *Augustusplatz*, the students shaped the cityscape. But can you erect a functional building in the same spot where the University Church St. Pauli was blown up in 1968? This was a topic of heated discussion. Suggestions covered anything from reconstruction, as the Dresden *Frauenkirche* experienced, to the audacious plans of German and international star architects. Also, the citizens of Leipzig courageously engaged in the discourse – the wounds of the blown up church still hurt.

UNIVERSITÄT LEIPZIG
1409
2009
ALMA MATER LIPSIENSIS

Signet zur 600-Jahr-Feier.
Signet for the 600th anniversary celebration.

Das neue Antlitz der Universität – entworfen vom niederländischen Architekten Erick van Egeraat.
The new face of the University, designed by the Dutch architect Erick van Egeraat.

Die Architekten Roland Bondzio (links) und Martin Behet im April 2007 auf der Campus-Baustelle.
The architects Roland Bondzio (left) and Martin Behet at the campus building site in April 2007.

HEFTIGE DEBATTEN

In einem international ausgeschriebenen Architektenwettbewerb zur Bebauung des Areals am Augustusplatz setzen sich die Architekten Martin Behet und Roland Bondzio mit ihren Entwürfen für Hörsaalkomplex, Seminargebäude, Mensa und das Institutsgebäude der Wirtschaftswissenschaftlichen Fakultät durch. Sie wollen den Campus nach außen mit Passagen und Durchgängen öffnen, Schwellen abbauen und den tristen Innenhof aus DDR-Tagen zum Leibniz-Forum umgestalten, wo sich Studenten, Wissenschaftler und Gäste gern treffen. Sie sehen den innerstädtischen Campus als lebendigen Stadtbaustein, der auch Historisches wie die bronzene Leibniz-Plastik und das Schinkeltor integriert. Eine rund um die Uhr geöffnete Bibliothek wie an amerikanischen Eliteuniversitäten soll künftig den Studenten nie dagewesenen Komfort bieten.

Ungeklärt bleibt zunächst die Frage, welche Architektursprache das Hauptgebäude und der Kirche-Aula-Bau tragen sollen. Es wird ein großer Wurf gesucht, der Geschichte und Anspruch der Universität Leipzig als international ausgerichtete, interdisziplinär agierende, zur Bürgerstadt hin offene Lehr- und Forschungsstätte ausdrückt. Gleichzeitig geht es um eine angemessene Erinnerung an die Zerstörung der Universitätskirche St. Pauli und des Augusteums. Die Universitätsleitung unter Rektor Volker Bigl, der von 1997 bis 2003 die Geschicke der Alma mater Lipsiensis führt, spricht sich von Anfang an gegen den originalen Wiederaufbau der zerstörten Universitätskirche aus. Man brauche keine potemkinschen Dörfer, sondern eine praktikable

HEATED DEBATES

In the international architectural invitation to tender for building upon the area at *Augustusplatz,* the architects Martin Behet und Roland Bondzio prevailed with their drafts for the lecture hall complex, seminar building, cafeteria and the institute building of the Faculty of Economics. These architects want to open the campus to the outside by using arcades and alleyways, removing barriers, and redesigning the dull inner court, dating back to GDR days, to become a Leibniz forum where students, scientists and guests will like to meet. Behet and Bondzio see the inner city campus as a living city block, which also integrates historical elements such as the bronze Leibniz sculpture and the Schinkel gate. A 24-hour library, similar to the American ivy league universities, will offer convenience to students which has been unheard of to this day.

The question as to which architectural language shall be expressed by the main building and the church/assembly hall building remained unsolved at first. A masterstroke was needed which expressed both history and the University of Leipzig's claim to be an internationally oriented, interdisciplinary teaching and research institution, open to the people of the city. It was also of consideration that the structure should be an adequate reminder of the destruction of the University Church St. Pauli and the Augusteum. The University Management under Rector Volker Bigl, who led the fate of the Alma mater Lipsiensis from 1997 to 2003, argued against the

Neue Zentralmensa gegenüber der Moritzbastei.
New central cafeteria opposite the Moritzbastei.

Blick von der Grimmaischen Straße (links) und von der Universitätsstraße auf den neuen Campus.
View of the new campus from the Grimmaische Straße *(left) and from the* Universitätsstraße.

Integration von Gottesdienstraum und Aula – schließlich muss die Universität seit 1943 auf einen Versammlungsort verzichten und hat bei Großveranstaltungen lediglich Gaststatus zum Beispiel im Gewandhaus.

Nach monatelangen, heftigen Debatten um die Neugestaltung des Campus und insbesondere des einstigen Paulinerkirchen-Areals rückt im Januar 2003 die Landesregierung von der Universität ab. Volker Bigl betrachtet dies als Vertrauensbruch und tritt spontan zurück, auch die Prorektoren Monika Krüger (Lehre und Studium), Helmut Papp (Forschung und wissenschaftlicher Nachwuchs) und Franz Häuser (Strukturelle Entwicklung) legen kurz darauf ihre Amtsgeschäfte nieder. Knapp drei Monate später wählt das Konzil den Professor für Bank- und Börsenrecht, Franz Häuser, zum neuen Rektor. Damals ahnt er noch nicht, dass er nicht nur für die verbleibende Amtszeit von einem guten halben Jahr, der Universität Leipzig vorstehen, sondern diese auch ins Jubiläum führen wird.

SPEKTAKULÄRER ENTWURF

Auch im Architekturstreit zeichnet sich eine Lösung ab. Im März 2004 kürt eine Jury den spektakulären Entwurf des Architekten Erick van Egeraat zum Wettbewerbssieger. Die Philosophie des Niederländers besteht im Bekenntnis zur Historie und zugleich in einem mutigen Schritt nach vorn. Er nimmt Anleihen von der Universitätskirche St. Pauli und integriert diese in ein multifunktionales Gebäude. Das Paulinum, so der Name des Neubaus, wird künftig neben einer Aula für akademische Feiern, wissenschaftliche Dispute und Konzerte auch einen großzügigen Raum mit dem Titel »Universitätskirche St. Pauli« für Gottesdienste bieten. Ein dem Original nachempfundenes Deckenkreuzgewölbe und mehrere Lichtsäulen im Inneren, eine

original reconstruction of the destroyed University Church right from the outset. Smoke and mirrors were not required, but a feasible integration of church service room and assembly hall – the University had had to do without an assembly hall since 1943 after all, and had only maintained a guest status for large events, for instance in the *Gewandhaus* concert hall.

After month-long heated debates about the new design of the campus and, in particular, the former *Pauliner* Church plot, the State Government suddenly disavowed the University. Volker Bigl considered this a breach of trust and spontaneously stepped down. Also the Prorectors Monika Krüger (Teaching and study), Helmut Papp (Research and junior scientists) and Franz Häuser (Structural development) resigned from their official functions immediately thereafter. The *Konzil* elected the professor of banking and stock exchange law, Franz Häuser, to be the new Rector, scarcely three months later. He would not know at that point, that he would preside over the University for the remaining term of office of half a year, and also lead it into its jubilee year.

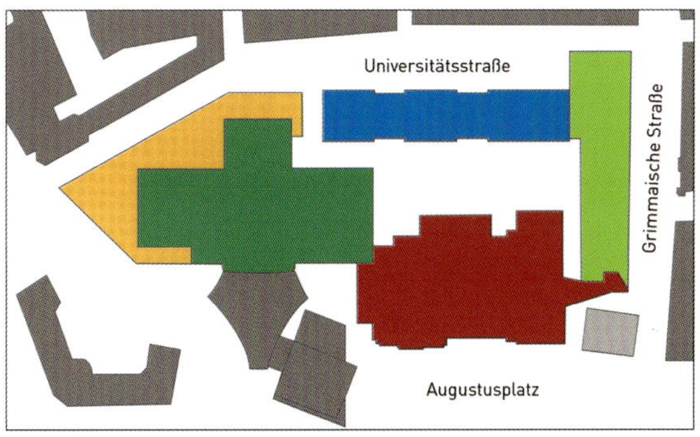

Der Campus im Überblick:
Overview of the campus:

- ***Paulinum, Neues Augusteum und Auditorium Maximum*** *Paulinum, New Augusteum and Auditorium Maximum*
- ***Institutsgebäude*** *Institute building*
- ***Seminargebäude*** *Seminar building*
- ***Hörsaalgebäude*** *Lecture hall building*
- ***Zentralmensa*** *Central cafeteria*
- ***Nicht zur Universität gehörende Bausubstanz*** *Structures not belonging to the University.*
- ***Café Felsche*** *Café Felsche*

Architekt Erick van Egeraat mit seinem Siegermodell für den neuen Campus.
Architect Erick van Egeraat and his winning model of the new campus.

Rechts: Die Universitätsbaustelle am Augustusplatz im Sommer 2008.
Right: The University building site at the Augustusplatz square in summer 2008.

Rosette an der Frontseite und ein Glockenturm mit der 1659 gegossenen Bronzeglocke der Universität stehen für die architektonische Tradition. Ein Lichtschlitz, der sich vom Boden hinweg durch die übrigen acht Stockwerke bis zum Dach zieht, greift den barbarischen Akt der Sprengung von 1968 auf. Egeraat will nicht kopieren, sondern erinnern, weicher und reicher bauen als es in den vergangenen Jahrzehnten üblich war.

Am 15. Juli 2005 legen Rektor Franz Häuser, Ministerpräsident Georg Milbradt und Wissenschaftsministerin Barbara Ludwig den Grundstein für den rund 200 Millionen Euro teuren Campus. Anfang 2007

Abschied vom alten Hauptgebäude: Rektor Franz Häuser im Schneetreiben am 8. Februar 2007.
Departing from the old main building: Rector Franz Häuser in blowing snow on 8 February 2007.

SPECTACULAR DESIGN

A solution to the architects' dispute began to present itself: a jury elected the spectacular design by the Dutch architect Erick van Egeraat to be the winner of the competition in March 2004. His philosophy consisted of a commitment to history and, at the same time, it was a courageous step forward. He borrowed elements of the University Church St. Pauli and integrated them into a multi purpose building. The new building – the Paulinum – will offer a generous room called "University Church St. Pauli" for church services, in addition to an assembly hall for academic celebrations, academic debates and concerts. A ceiling cross-vault, based on the original church, several light columns in the interior, a rosetta at the front and a belfry housing the bronze bell of the University, originally cast in 1659, will be representative of the architectural tradition. A slit, extending from the ground through the remaining eight storeys up to the roof, will allow light to shine through, and is symbolic of the act of barbarism committed when the church was blown up in 1968. Egeraat does not want to duplicate, but rather to commemorate and build in a softer and richer way than was usual in the past decades.

On 15 July 2005, Rector Franz Häuser, State Prime Minister Georg Milbradt and Minister of Science and Research Barbara Ludwig laid the cornerstone for the campus, which will cost about 200 million euros. At the beginning of 2007, a new leaf in University building history was turned over: the lights went out in the main building, the paternoster lift travelled for the last time and the excavator arm dug its way, storey by storey, through the concrete. A certain sadness combined with anticipation of the new. But the building schedule is tight. Actually, the campus is to be completely ready for the 600th anniversary of the founding of the University on 2 December 2009. As we approach that date, the more it becomes obvious that completion of the building may extend beyond that target date. The motivation, however, of construction workers, University staff and citizens is high. When the University invited the public to its open

wird dann ein neues Kapitel baulicher Universitätsgeschichte aufgeschlagen: Im Hauptgebäude gehen die Lichter aus, der Paternoster fährt ein letztes Mal, Greifarme von Baggern fressen sich Stockwerk für Stockwerk durch den Beton. Wehmut kehrt ein – und die Vorfreude auf Neues. Doch der Zeitplan ist eng. Eigentlich soll der Campus zum 600. Gründungstag der Universität am 2. Dezember 2009 vollständig fertig sein. Monat für Monat zeichnet sich immer deutlicher ab, dass es eine Fertigstellung auf Raten wird. Doch die Motivation bei Bauleuten, Universitätsangehörigen und Bürgern ist hoch. Als die Universität Ende 2008 zum Tag der offenen Tür lädt, strömen binnen weniger Stunden mehr als 6 000 begeisterte Interessenten auf die Baustelle. Und Sachsens Ministerpräsident Stanislaw Tillich macht im Frühjahr 2009 Mut: »Zur Not feiern wir in Gummistiefeln.«

ERSTE LORBEEREN

Der Nachholbedarf ostdeutscher Hochschulen gegenüber jenen in den alten Bundesländern ist groß. Die Universität Leipzig als klassische Volluniversität ist breit aufgestellt. Das wissenschaftliche Fächerspektrum reicht von Geistes- und Sozialwissenschaften über Medizin und Veterinärmedizin bis hin zu äußerst ertragreichen Naturwissenschaften, die interdisziplinär zusammenarbeiten, sich gegenseitig anregen und entwickeln. Grenzüberschreitungen zwischen den herkömmlichen wissenschaftlichen Disziplinen,

door day at the end of 2008, more than 6,000 enthusiastic, interested people swarmed onto the building site within just a few hours. And Saxony's Prime Minister Stanislaw Tillich encouraged in spring 2009: "If need be, we celebrate in rubber boots."

FIRST LAURELS

The backlog demand for East German higher education institutions compared to those in the old federal states was great. The University of Leipzig as a classical full university is broadly positioned: the academic spectrum of courses stretches from the humanities and social sciences to medicine and veterinary medicine and high-yield natural sciences, which cooperate on an interdisciplinary basis and inspire and further one another. The crossing of boundaries between the conventional academic disciplines, international cooperation, interrelationship between science and economy – both regionally and internationally – are not only tradition at the University, but also the foundation of its academic excellence at the beginning of the 21st century.

First laurels – and thus motivation for their further work – were harvested by researchers in the years 2007 and 2008: the graduate school BuildMoNa won the Federal Excellence Initiative. And the research programme "LIFE: Leipzig Interdisciplinary Research Cluster of Genetic Factors, Clinical Phenotypes and Environment" at the University is supported with the

Modell des Andachtsraumes im neuen Paulinum.
Model of the devotions room in the new Paulinum.

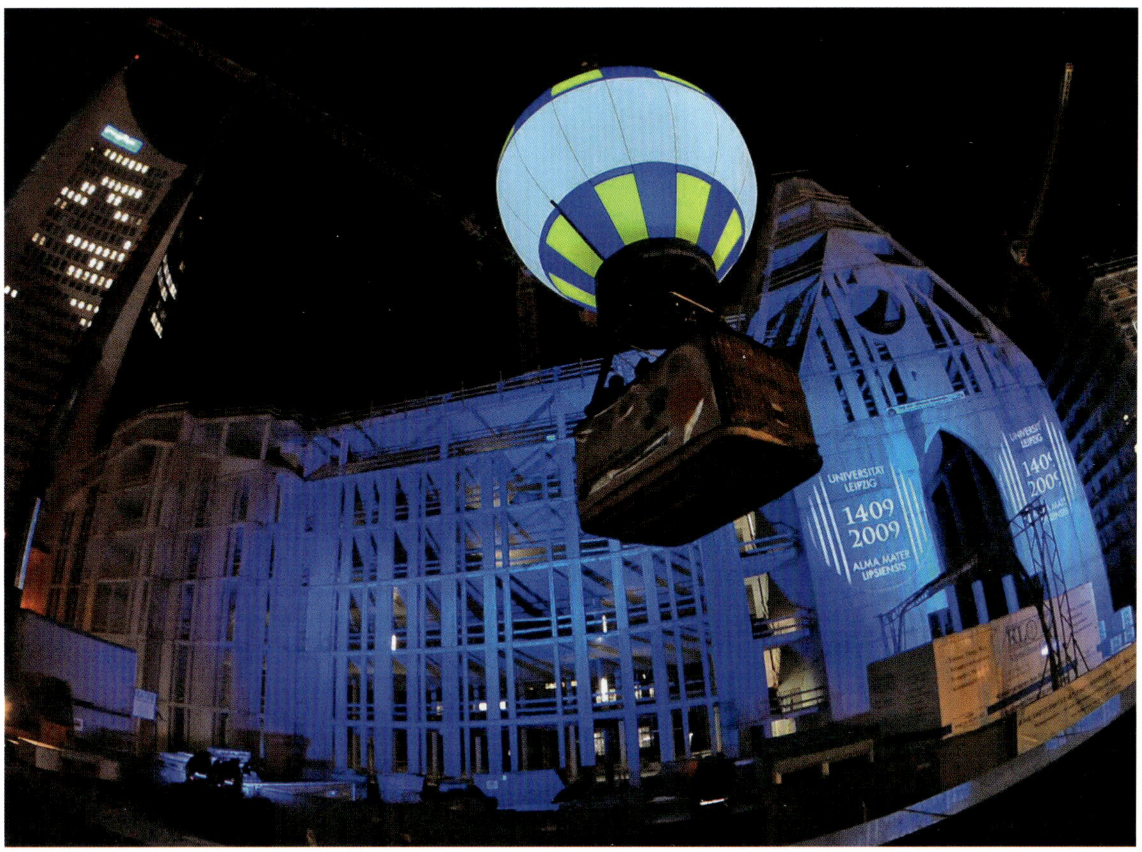

Tag der offenen Baustelle am 2. Dezember 2008.
Building site open to the public on 2 December 2008.

Jubiläumsschau »Kosmos des Wissens« in der Bibliotheca Albertina.
Anniversary exhibition "Cosmos of Knowledge" at the Bibliotheca Albertina.

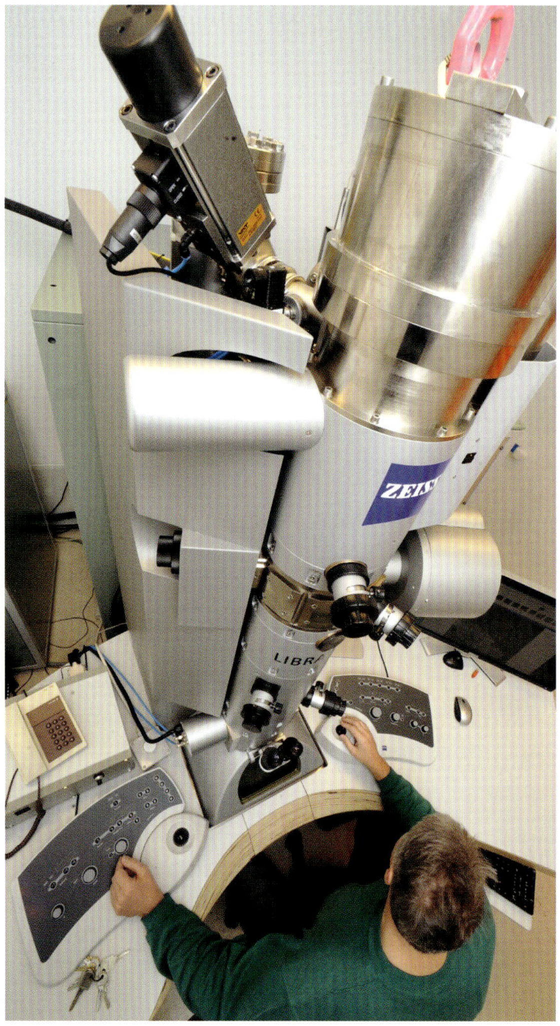

Rechts: Elektronenmikroskop an der Veterinärmedizinischen Fakultät.
Right: Electron microscope at the Faculty of Veterinary Medicine.

internationale Kooperationen, die Vernetzung von Wissenschaft und Wirtschaft – sowohl regional als auch international – sind nicht nur Tradition der Universität, sondern auch die Grundlage ihrer wissenschaftlichen Exzellenz Anfang des 21. Jahrhunderts.

Erste Lorbeeren – und damit eine Motivation für die weitere Arbeit – ernten die Forscher in den Jahren 2007 und 2008: Die Graduiertenschule BuildMoNa siegt in der Bundesexzellenzinitiative. Und in der Exzellenzinitiative des Freistaates wird an der Universität das Forschungsprogramm »LIFE: Leipzig Interdisciplinary Research Cluster of Genetic Factors, Clinical Phenotypes and Environment (Leipziger Interdisziplinärer Forschungskomplex zu molekularen Ursachen umwelt- und lebensstilassoziierter Erkrankungen)« mit dem landesweit höchsten Einzelbetrag in Höhe von 38 Millionen Euro bis 2013 gefördert. Und: 2007 wird die 60-Millionen-Euro-Marke an Drittmitteln für die Forschung erstmals überschritten.

Die 456 Professoren begrenzen ihr wissenschaftliches Wirken jedoch nicht allein auf die Universität. Die Kontakte der Hochschullehrer und Forscher gehen in jedem einzelnen Fach weit darüber hinaus. Durch die Überschreitung der Fakultätsgrenzen und in Zusammenarbeit mit außeruniversitären Forschungseinrichtungen lassen sich die unterschiedlichen Projekte deutlich besser betreuen und vernetzen. Drei Leibniz-Institute, drei Max-Planck-Institute, zwei Fraunhofer-Institute und das Helmholtz-Zentrum für Umweltforschung bieten eine hervorragende Infrastruktur für Forschung und Studium. Ein vielfältiges fachübergreifendes Qualifikationsprogramm für Doktoranden offeriert auch die 2006 gegründete Research Academy.

PROFILBILDENDE BEREICHE

Schon 2004 hat sich die Universität entschieden, ihr Forschungsprofil durch den Aufbau von Profilbildenden Forschungsbereichen zu schärfen und gleichzeitig eine balancierte Vielfalt zu erhalten. »Von Molekülen und Nanoobjekten zu multifunktionalen Materialien und Prozessen« heißt der erste von sechs Profilbildenden Forschungsbereichen. Gesucht werden neue Arten der Kommunikation, die auf Basis der

highest single amount throughout the state, of 38 million euros, within the Excellence Initiative of the Free State of Saxony, until 2013. And in 2007 the threshold of 60 million euros in third-party funds for research was exceeded for the first time.

The 456 professors do not limit their academic activities to the University, the contacts of the lecturers and researchers go far beyond in each individual field. By the crossing of faculty boundaries and in cooperation with research institutions outside the University, the several projects can be overseen and interrelated in a far better way. Three Leibniz Institutes, three Max Planck Institutes, two Fraunhofer Institutes and the Helmholtz Centre for Environmental Research offer an outstanding infrastructure for research and study. The Research Academy, founded in 2006, offers a manifold interdisciplinary qualification programme for doctoral candidates as well.

TOP-LEVEL RESEARCH AREAS

The University decided as early as 2004 to enhance its research profile by setting up top-level research areas and, at the same time, by maintaining a balanced

Links: Seminar im Geisteswissenschaftlichen Zentrum.
Left: Seminar in the Centre for the Humanities.

Vietnamesische Studenten bei der praktischen Ausbildung im Labor.
Vietnamese students while training in the lab.

Nanotechnologie eine weitgehende Immunität gegen Abhörmechanismen garantieren. Chemiker, Physiker, Biologen und Angehörige vieler technischen Disziplinen erforschen dabei die Welt der kleinsten Teilchen, von ein bis etwa 100 Nanometer. Zum Vergleich: Ein menschliches Haar hat einen Durchmesser von etwa 10 Mikrometern, das sind 10 000 Nanometer. Ein Virus hat eine Größe von rund 30 Nanometern.

In der Graduiertenschule BuildMoNa (Building with Molecules and Nano-objects – Bauen mit Molekülen und Nanoobjekten), mit der sich die Universität als einzige sächsische Hochschule 2007 bei der zweiten Runde der Bundesexzellenzinitiative behaupten kann und nun gefördert wird, erforschen international

variety of subjects. "Multifunctional materials and processes from molecules and nanodevices" is the first of six top-level research areas. New types of communication are required, which, based on nanotechnology, assure extensive immunity against bugging mechanisms. Chemists, physicists, biologists and those affiliated with many technical disciplines explore the world of micro particles, measuring about one to about 100 nanometers. In comparison, a human hair has a diameter of about 10 micrometers, that is, approximately 10,000 nanometers. A virus measures about 30 nanometers.

International, highly gifted doctoral candidates explore, together with established scientists, new classes

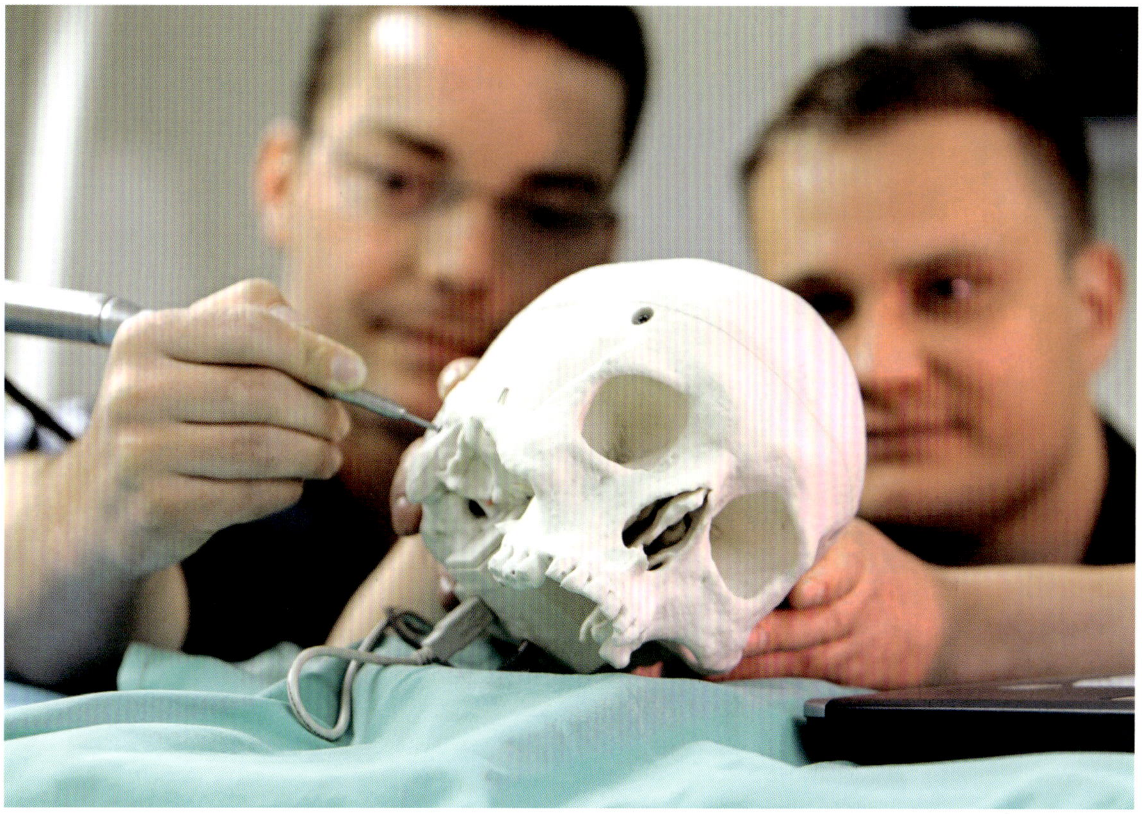

Modell zur Simulation von Operationen am menschlichen Schädel.
Model for simulating operations on the human skull.

Universität der kurzen Wege: Geisteswissenschaftliches Zentrum, Bibliothek (rechts) und erholsame Grünanlagen.
University of short distances: Centre for the Humanities, library (right) and relaxing green spaces.

Eulersche Zahl am Hörsaal der Fakultät für Chemie und Mineralogie.
Euler's number (the mathematical constant e) at the lecture hall of the Faculty of Chemistry and Mineralogy.

hochbegabte Doktoranden gemeinsam mit etablierten Wissenschaftlern neuartige Formen von Werkstoffen, die den Bauprinzipien aktiver, lebender Materie folgen. Ein abstraktes Forschungsfeld, dass aber unter anderem in der Tumorforschung praktische Anwendung findet.

Ausgehend von evolutionsbiologischen und bioinformatischen Ansätzen werden im Profilbildenden Forschungsbereich »Molekulare und zelluläre Kommunikation: Biotechnologie, Bioinformatik und Biomedizin in Therapie und Diagnostik« die Materialwissenschaften mit den Ansätzen der Zelltherapie kombiniert. Ein Schwerpunkt ist die Geweberegeneration. Angestrebt wird die reibungslose Überführung von klinisch relevanten Resultaten aus der Grundlagenforschung in klinische Studien sowie eine verbesserte Diagnostik, Therapie und Prävention.

Im Profilbildenden Forschungsbereich »Gehirn, Kognition und Sprache« untersuchen Mediziner sowie Natur- und Geisteswissenschaftler höhere geistige Funktionen wie Aufmerksamkeit, Wahrnehmung, Lernen, Gedächtnis, Motorik und Sprache, um so wertvolle Hinweise bei Hirnerkrankungen zu

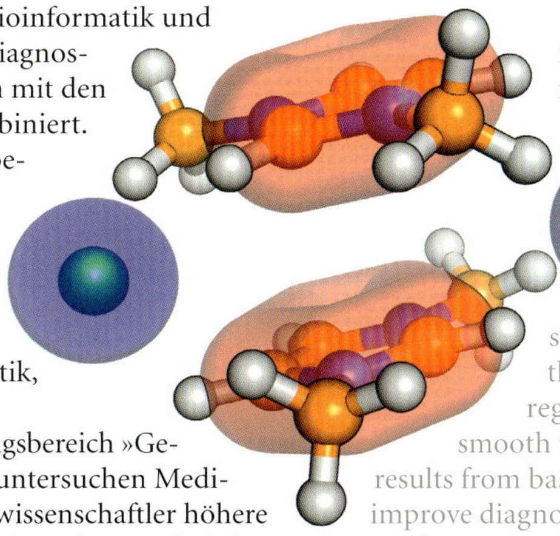

Grafische Darstellung ionischer Flüssigkeiten.
Graphic depiction of ionic liquids.

of materials that follow the structuring principles of active, living matter, at the graduate school BuildMoNa (Building with Molecules and Nano-objects). An abstract research area, which is, for instance, applied in tumor research. With BuildMoNa, the University was the only institution of higher education in Saxony to stand its ground in the second heat of the Federal Excellence Initiative in 2007, and now receives funding.

Based on evolutionary and bioinformatic approaches, the top-level research area "Molecular and Cellular Communication: Biotechnology, Bioinformatics and Biomedicine in Therapy and Diagnostics" combines materials science with the approaches of cell therapy, with an emphasis on tissue regeneration. The aims are to effect a smooth transition of clinically relevant results from basic research to clinical trials and to improve diagnosis, therapy and prevention.

In the top-level research area "Brain, Cognition and Language" physicians and academics from the natural sciences and the humanities investigate higher

Blick auf das Medizinische Viertel entlang der Liebigstraße.
View of the Medical Quarter along the Liebigstraße.

gewinnen. Sie fokussieren präventive und therapeutische Heilungsmethoden, die bei einer immer älter werdenden Bevölkerung und damit rapide ansteigenden Zahl von Schlaganfällen, Demenz, Parkinson und Depression dringend benötigt werden.

Bei der Entstehung von Zivilisationskrankheiten, zu denen auch Arteriosklerose, Allergien und Tumoren zählen, spielen Umweltbelastungen und Lebensstile eine erhebliche Rolle, wie die Mitglieder des Profilbildenden Forschungsbereichs »Veränderte Umwelt und Krankheit« wissen. Der Einfluss genomischer und molekularer Faktoren zusammen mit Umwelt und Lebensstil auf Entstehung und Verlauf dieser Krankheiten ist medizinisch von hoher Bedeutung, jedoch nur unzureichend geklärt. Dieses Manko wollen die Wissenschaftler gemeinsam mit außeruniversitären Forschungseinrichtungen beseitigen.

Im Profilbildenden Bereich »Mathematik und ihre Anwendung in den Naturwissenschaften« wird schwerpunktmäßig auf dem Gebiet struktureller Probleme

cognitive functions like attention, apperception, learning, memory, motor function and language, in order to gain valuable insights for brain-related diseases. They focus on preventive and therapeutic healing methods, which are urgently needed, given an ever aging population and, consequently, a rapidly growing number of strokes and cases of dementia, Parkinson's disease and depression.

Environmental pollution and lifestyles play an essential part in the development of diseases of civilization, such as arteriosclerosis, allergies and tumors, as scientists of the top-level research area "Environmental Changes and Diseases" recognize. The influence of genomic and molecular factors, combined with environment and lifestyle, contributing to the development and progress of these diseases is of high medical relevance, but insufficiently explored. The scientists want, together with research institutions outside the University, to overcome this deficiency.

Links: Vorbereitung im Labor auf eine Experimental-Vorlesung im Hörsaal.
Left: Preparation in the lab for a presentation of experiments in the lecture hall.

geforscht, die direkt aus physikalischen, inzwischen auch immer mehr biologischen Fragestellungen erwachsen. Die Mathematik ist dabei das verbindende Element der beteiligten Forscher des vor 125 Jahren von Felix Klein gegründeten Instituts für Mathematik, des Instituts für Theoretische Physik und des 1996 in Leipzig etablierten Max-Planck-Instituts für Mathematik in den Naturwissenschaften. Das gemeinsame Projekt wird von der Überzeugung getragen, dass die auftretenden Probleme nicht durch die Anwendung existierender mathematischer Verfahren gelöst werden können, sondern neue Mathematik erfordern.

Die politikwissenschaftlich, historisch-philosophische Frage nach »Riskanten Ordnungen« steht im Mittelpunkt des sechsten Profilbildenden Forschungsbereichs. Dabei geht es im Kern um die Veränderung der politischen Systeme in Zeiten von Finanzkrisen,

The top-level research-area "Mathematics and its application in natural sciences" focusses on research in the field of the structural problems arising directly from physical and increasingly biological questions. Mathematics is the linking element between the researchers of the Institute of Mathematics, founded by Felix Klein 125 years ago, the Institute of Theoretical Physics and the Max Planck Institute of Mathematics in the Natural Sciences, established in Leipzig in 1996. The common project bears the conviction that the problems emerging cannot be solved by applying existing mathematical methods, but instead require new mathematics.

The political science and historical-philosophical question for "Contested Orders" is at the centre of the sixth top-level research area. At its core is the shift in political systems in times of financial crises, natural disasters and terrorism. Researchers explore the question of how should a government be thinking today in order to cope with challenges that repeatedly and unexpectedly affect it.

EUROPEAN CHALLENGE

When 30 European states signed the Bologna declaration in June 1999, they had one aim: they wanted to create a common European Higher Education Area and reform the inconsistent heterogeneous higher education system to create degrees that are on a comparable level throughout Europe. Soon it became obvious: *Magister* and *Diplom* were things of the past and the newly graded degrees are called Bachelor and Master. The Bachelor will lead students to a degree in

Knuddeliges Souvenir: der Diplombär.
Cuddly souvenir: the diploma bear.

Mikroskopiersaal an der Medizinischen Fakultät.
Microscopy hall at the Faculty of Medicine.

Naturkatastrophen und Terrorismus. Die Forscher gehen der Frage nach, wie eine Regierung heute denken muss, um den Herausforderungen, die immer wieder unerwartet auf sie einwirken, gewachsen zu sein.

Rechts: Geschäftszentrum Petersbogen mit Juridicum-Passage in der Innenstadt.
Right: Petersbogen *business centre with Juridicum arcades in the inner city.*

EUROPÄISCHE HERAUSFORDERUNG

Als 30 europäische Staaten im Juni 1999 die Bologna-Erklärung unterzeichnen, haben sie ein Ziel: Sie wollen einen gemeinsamen europäischen Hochschulraum schaffen und das uneinheitliche Hochschulwesen reformieren, um europaweit vergleichbare Studienabschlüsse zu schaffen. Rasch wird klar: Magister und Diplom sind Auslaufmodelle, die neuen gestaffelten Abschlüsse heißen Bachelor und Master. Der Bachelor soll die Studenten bereits nach drei bis vier Jahren zu einem Abschluss führen, damit die jungen Akademiker früher als bisher in die Berufswelt einsteigen können. Vor allem aber ist dieses Studiensystem international kompatibel und bildet damit die Grundlage für mehr Mobilität im Studium. Die konkrete Zulassung zur zweiten Stufe, einem Masterstudiengang, hängt auch von den Leistungen im Bachelor-Studium ab.

Die Universität Leipzig stellt als eine der ersten Hochschulen bundesweit zum Wintersemester 2006/07 ihr Studiensystem komplett auf insgesamt 115 Bachelor- und Masterstudiengänge um. »Dies ist die größte Reform seit Humboldt«, sagt Rektor Franz Häuser über die Herausforderungen für akademische Verwaltung, Lehrende und Studenten. Das Studienangebot reicht von A wie Afrikanistik bis Z wie Zahnmedizin, reagiert auch mit den fächerübergreifenden European Studies auf die wachsende Europäische Union und

In sechs Semestern zum Bachelor.
Six semesters to a Bachelor's degree.

as little as three to four years and enable the young academics to enter the working world sooner. Above all, this study system is internationally compatible and forms the basis for more mobility during study. The actual admission to the second stage, a Master's degree programme, depends also on one's performance in the Bachelor's programme.

Seminarpause im Park an der Moritzbastei.
A break between seminars in the park at Moritzbastei.

Offen für alle: Kinderuniversität und Seniorenkolleg.
Open to everyone: children's university and study for seniors.

bietet mit Sorabistik und Onomastik (Namenskunde) gefragte Alleinstellungsmerkmale.

Auch die Lehre hält Schritt: Im Herbst 2006 beginnt die Universität mit E-Learning, zwei Jahre später haben schon 12 000 Studenten einen Zugang zur neuen Form des Lernens und der Wissensvermittlung. Auch Skeptiker können rasch davon überzeugt werden, dass sich Lehrende und Lernende keineswegs nur noch virtuell begegnen, sondern dass das Angebot eine sinnvolle Mischung aus Präsenzlehre im Hörsaal und in Seminaren sowie dem computergestützten Lernen zuhause ist. Mit Tastatur und Bildschirm statt Füller und Papier, lautet die Devise. Die Lehre soll dadurch weiter verbessert, die Kommunikation zwischen Professoren und Studenten vereinfacht werden. So können die Lehrkräfte zum Beispiel Sprechstundentermine auf elektronischem Weg vereinbaren oder Fristen für die

The University of Leipzig was one of the first institutions of higher education throughout Germany to switch its degree system completely to include a total of 115 Bachelor's and Master's programmes in the winter semester 2006/7. "This has been the largest reform since Humboldt", said Rector Franz Häuser about the challenge for academic administration, teaching staff and students. The programmes and courses offered stretch from A to Z (African studies to Zoology). Interdisciplinary European studies address the growing European Union and provide unique course offerings, that are highly in demand, such as Sorbian studies and onomastics (origin of names).

Teaching kept pace with those developments as well: in autumn 2006 the University began offering E-Learning. Two years later, this new form of learning and imparting knowledge would become available to

November 2008 eröffnetes Studenten-Service-Zentrum in der Goethestraße.
Student service centre, opened in November 2008, in the Goethestraße.

Rechts: Andrang bei der feierlichen Immatrikulation im Oktober 2006 im Gewandhaus.
Right: Well attended, festive enrolment at the Gewandhaus *concert hall in October 2006.*

Studienberatung beim Tag der offenen Tür 2006.
Academic advising on the open door day in 2006.

Abgabe von Arbeiten zuteilen, ohne jedem einzelnen Studenten eine E-Mail schreiben zu müssen.

Zeitgemäße Studiengänge, neue Gebäude, sichtbare Forschungserfolge – die Universität Leipzig hat die Lücke nach 40 Jahren deutsch-deutscher Teilung binnen kürzester Zeit geschlossen und strebt an die Spitze

as many as 12,000 students. Sceptics would soon be convinced that teachers and students would by no means meet only virtually, but that students could combine a meaningful mix of traditional classroom learning and computer assisted learning at home – the motto being: with keyboard and monitor instead of pen and paper. By using these methods, teaching is to be further improved, and communication between professors and students simplified; and those teaching can, for instance, electronically schedule appointments according to their available office hours, or they can assign deadlines for handing in papers without having to e-mail each student individually.

Within a very short time, modern courses of study, new buildings and visible success in research have enabled the University of Leipzig to bridge the gap after

Studentische Plakat-Aktion im Januar 2009.
Student poster initiative in January 2009.

Absolvententreffen im Rektoratsgebäude.
Meeting of graduates in the Rector's Office building.

deutscher Forschung und Lehre. Die Erfolgsgeschichte soll weitergeschrieben werden, der Grundstein dafür ist gelegt. Wie alle Hochschulen ist auch die Universität Leipzig im 21. Jahrhundert Teil einer globalen geistigen Kultur und zugleich fest in nationale wie internationale Ausbildungssysteme einbezogen. Sie ist aus der Geschichte erwachsen und Teil einer Zukunft, die sie weit überragt, getreu dem Leitmotto der Alma mater Lipsiensis »Aus Tradition Grenzen überschreiten«.

PROMINENTE ABSOLVENTEN

Wie attraktiv die Universität heute ist, beweisen rund 2 600 ausländische Studenten aus 150 Ländern der Welt und Hunderte ausländische Gastwissenschaftler, die jedes Jahr nach Leipzig kommen. Die Studentin mit der weitesten Anreise legte rund 23 500 Kilometer zurück. Mehr als 300 Hochschulpartnerschaften im Rahmen des Erasmus-Programms der Europäischen Union – benannt nach dem Humanisten Erasmus von Rotterdam – und eine Vielzahl von Fakultätspartnerschaften bieten umfangreiche Austauschmöglichkeiten. Und jeder einzelne Absolvent und jeder ehemalige Mitarbeiter ist als Alumnus oder Alumna ein Botschafter »seiner« Alma mater im In- und Ausland.

Zeigte man die Leipziger Alumni als Punkte auf einer Landkarte, so wären diese in Deutschland dicht gesät, aber auch über den ganzen Erdball leicht aufzufinden. Zu den prominentesten

Die Tasse zum Jubiläum.
The anniversary cup.

40 years of German separation. The University aspires to the top rank in German teaching and research. The success story is to be continued and the foundation has been laid. As all institutions of higher learning in the 21st century, the University of Leipzig is part of a global, intellectual culture and, at the same time, firmly integrated in both national and international education systems. It has risen out of history and is now moving towards the future, faithful to the guiding principle of the Alma mater Lipsiensis "A Tradition of Crossing Boundaries".

ILLUSTRIOUS GRADUATES

About 2,600 international students from 150 countries around the world and hundreds of international visiting researchers annually, prove the popularity of the University today. The student who had the longest journey, covered 23,500 km on her way to Leipzig. More than 300 academic partnerships within the Erasmus programme of the European Union – named after the humanist Erasmus von Rotterdam – and a variety of faculty partnerships offer extensive exchange opportunities. And every single graduate and former staff, as alumni, is an ambassador of the University in Germany and abroad.

If one showed Leipzig alumni as dots on a map, they would be densely packed in Germany, but easily located around the globe as well. The most illustrious

Haupteingang zum 2002 eröffneten Neubau für die Geistes- und Sozialwissenschaften.
Main entrance to the new building for humanities and social sciences, opened in 2002.

Absolventen der Gegenwart zählen Bundeskanzlerin Angela Merkel (Physik), der ehemalige Bundesaußenminister und Ehrendoktor der Juristenfakultät, Hans-Dietrich Genscher, und Sachsen-Anhalts Ministerpräsident Wolfgang Böhmer (Medizin). Aber auch Schriftsteller wie Christa Wolf, Volker Braun, Juli Zeh und Clemens Meyer sowie TV-Moderatoren wie Kristin Otto und Maybritt Illner lernten ihr Handwerk an der Universität Leipzig. Gerne erinnern sich auch die ausländischen Alumni an ihre Leipziger Studienzeit: Die chilenische Präsidentin Verónica Michelle Bachelet lernte am Herder-Institut Deutsch als Fremdsprache, der Parlamentspräsident der Republik Kap Verde, Aristides Raimundo Lima, studierte Rechtswissenschaften, der polnische Botschafter in der Bundesrepublik, Marek Prawda, war Student der Wirtschaftswissenschaften und der mongolische Schriftsteller Galsan Tschinag für Germanistik eingeschrieben.

graduates of the present day include Federal Chancellor Angela Merkel (Physics), the former Federal Minister for Foreign Affairs and honorary doctor of the Faculty of Law, Hans-Dietrich Genscher, and the Prime Minister of Saxony-Anhalt, Wolfgang Böhmer (Medicine). Also writers such as Christa Wolf, Volker Braun, Juli Zeh and Clemens Meyer, and TV-presenters Kristin Otto and Maybritt Illner learned their craft at the University of Leipzig. International alumni voluntarily reflect back on their student days in Leipzig as well: the Chilean President Verónica Michelle Bachelet studied German as a foreign language at the Herder-Institute; the Speaker of the Parliament of the Republic Kap Verde, Aristides Raimundo Lima, studied law; the Polish Ambassador to the Federal Republic, Marek Prawda, was enrolled as a student of economics, and the Mongolian writer Galsan Tschinag in German studies.

Links: Studio von Uni-Radio »mephisto 97.6«.
Left: Studio at the University radio station "mephisto 97.6".

Punktspiel der »Uni-Riesen« (weiß) vom Universitätssportclub USC.
League game of the "Uni-Riesen" (white) of the University sports club.

DIE ZUKUNFT BEGINNT

Die 600-Jahr-Feier 2009 ist für die Universität eine wichtige Etappe in der Geschichte und steht in einer langen Tradition. 1609 erinnerte sich die Alma mater erstmals bewusst ihrer Anfänge und zelebrierte das Datum des Gründungstages mit einem Festakt. Am 2. Dezember wurde in der jüngsten Vergangenheit der »dies academicus« zu einem festen Ritual – und ist es bis heute. Die bislang größte Feier gab es zum 500. Universitätsjubiläum. Delegationen und Abgeordnete aus der ganzen Welt reisten dazu nach Leipzig, 180 kostbare und künstlerisch aufwändig gestaltete Glückwunschadressen aus aller Welt sowie 170 wertvolle

THE FUTURE BEGINS

The 600 year celebration is for the University an important stage in history and part of a long tradition. In 1609 the Alma mater commemorated, for the first time, its beginnings and celebrated the date of its foundation with a ceremonial act. In the recent past the "dies academicus" on 2 December has become a firm ritual – and still is today. The biggest celebration so far took place at the 500th anniversary of the University. Delegations and deputies from the whole world travelled to Leipzig then. 180 valuable and extensively decorated congratulatory messages from all over the world and 170 valuable, non-monetary

Chor und Orchester der Universität im Gewandhaus.
Choir and orchestra of the University at the Gewandhaus concert hall.

Das Rektoratskollegium im Jubiläumsjahr 2009 (von links): Robert Holländer (Strukturelle Entwicklung), Frank Nolden (Kanzler), Franz Häuser (Rektor), Wolfgang Fach (Lehre und Studium), Martin Schlegel (Forschung und wissenschaftlicher Nachwuchs).
University Management in the anniversary year 2009 (from left): Robert Holländer (Structural development), Frank Nolden (Head of administration), Franz Häuser (Rector), Wolfgang Fach (Teaching and study), Martin Schlegel (Research and junior scientists).

Sachgeschenke erreichten die Universität. Ein Festgottesdienst in der Paulinerkirche eröffnete die Feierlichkeiten, die mit einem Festzug von rund 2 500 Studenten am nächsten Tag endeten. Für den Kommers mit rund 10 000 Ehrengästen entstand sogar eine Festhalle, in der ein eigens kreiertes Jubiläumsbier ausgeschenkt wurde und die Reichspost eine Filiale eingerichtet hatte, um die Kartengrüße entgegenzunehmen.

Zu den Feierlichkeiten 2009 ist die Zahl der Ehrengäste beim Eröffnungskonzert am 9. Mai im Gewandhaus und beim akademischen Festakt am 2. Dezember im Paulinum sogar noch höher. Der geistige Maßstab allerdings hat sich verändert, im Mittelpunkt steht – ganz in der Tradition universitären Wirkens – die Auseinandersetzung mit der »universitas« und ihren Disziplinen. Mehr als 300 internationale Kongresse, Konzerte, Ausstellungen, allen voran die Jubiläumsausstellung »Erleuchtung der Welt. Sachsen und der Beginn der modernen Wissenschaften« im Alten Rathaus, demonstrieren die Vielfältigkeit der Wissenschaft einer klassischen Volluniversität. Das Motto der Alma mater Lipsiensis »Aus Tradition Grenzen überschreiten« ist dabei Programm, verdeutlicht die Schwerpunkte der Profilbildenden Forschungsbereiche, knüpft an den Erfolg bei den Exzellenzinitiativen von Bund und Land an – und weist den Weg in die Zukunft.

Gedenkmedaille zum Universitätsjubiläum.
Commemorative medal for the University anniversary.

gifts were given to the University. A festival service in *Pauliner* Church opened the celebrations, which ended in a procession of about 2,500 students on the following day. On the occasion of the commercium, attended by about 10,000 guests of honour, a festive hall was built in which anniversary beer especially created for the occasion was served. Also, the imperial postal service had set up an outlet in order to receive the greeting cards.

The number of honorary guests at the opening concert in the *Gewandhaus* on 9 May and at the ceremonial act in the Paulinum on 2 December, will be even higher for the celebrations in 2009. The celebration profile, however, has changed. The debate on "universitas" and its disciplines takes centre stage – in the very tradition of university activity. More than 300 international congresses, concerts, exhibitions, first and foremost the anniversary exhibition "Enlightening the world. Saxony and the beginning of modern sciences" in the Old Townhall, demonstrate the academic variety at a classical full university. The guiding principle of the Alma mater Lipsiensis "A Tradition of Crossing Boundaries" says it all and highlights the focal points of top-level research areas, and success in Federal and State Excellence Initiatives – and points the way to the future.

Treppenaufgang in der von 1994 bis 2002 komplett rekonstruierten Universitätsbibliothek.
Staircase in the University library which was completely reconstructed from 1994 to 2002.

NOBELPREISTRÄGER AN DER UNIVERSITÄT
NOBEL PRIZE LAUREATES AT THE UNIVERSITY

Svante Arrhenius
Nobelpreis für Chemie 1903, Assistent am Institut von Wilhelm Ostwald in Leipzig.
Nobel Prize in Chemistry 1903, assistant at the institute of Wilhelm Ostwald in Leipzig.

Friedrich Bergius
Nobelpreis für Chemie 1931, schrieb von 1905 bis 1907 in Leipzig seine Doktorarbeit.
Nobel Prize in Chemistry 1931, wrote his thesis in Leipzig from 1905 to 1907.

Felix Bloch
Nobelpreis für Physik 1952, promovierte 1928 in Leipzig am Institut von Werner Heisenberg.
Nobel Prize in Physics 1952, received 1928 PhD from institute of Werner Heisenberg in Leipzig.

Carl Bosch
Nobelpreis für Chemie 1931, fertigte 1896 bis 1898 in Leipzig seine Dissertationsschrift an.
Nobel Prize in Chemistry 1931, wrote his thesis in Leipzig from 1896 to 1898.

Peter Debye
Nobelpreis für Chemie 1936, von 1927 bis 1934 in Leipzig Professor für Experimentalphysik.
Nobel Prize in Chemistry 1936, from 1927 to 1934 Professor of Experimental Physics in Leipzig.

Paul Ehrlich
Nobelpreis für Medizin 1908, studierte und promovierte an der Medizinischen Fakultät.
Nobel Prize in Medicine 1908, study and doctorate at the Faculty of Medicine.

Enrico Fermi
Nobelpreis für Physik 1938, legte Grundstein dafür 1928 mit Vortrag an Leipzigs Universität.
Nobel Prize in Physics 1938, initiated by a paper he presented at Leipzig University.

Haldan Hartline
Nobelpreis für Medizin 1967, mehrfache Arbeitsaufenthalte am Physikalischen Institut.
Nobel Prize in Medicine 1967, several working stays at the Institute of Physics.

Gerhart Hauptmann
Literaturnobelpreis 1912, erhielt wenige Jahre zuvor in Leipzig die Ehrendoktorwürde.
Nobel Prize in Literature 1912, received an honorary doctorate in Leipzig a few years earlier.

Werner Heisenberg
Nobelpreis für Physik 1932, von 1927 bis 1942 in Leipzig Professor für Theoretische Physik.
Nobel Prize in Physics 1932, Professor of Theoretical Physics in Leipzig from 1927 to 1942.

Gustav Hertz
Nobelpreis für Physik 1925, leitete nach dem Zweiten Weltkrieg das Physikalische Institut.
Nobel Prize in Physics 1925, led the Institute of Physics after the Second World War.

Jacobus H. van't Hoff
Nobelpreis für Chemie 1901, gab mit Wilhelm Ostwald in Leipzig eine Zeitschrift heraus.
Nobel Prize in Chemistry 1901, co-published journal with Wilhelm Ostwald in Leipzig.

Bernard Katz
Nobelpreis für Medizin 1970, Leipziger, 1929 Studium, 1934 Doktor, 1990 Ehrendoktor.
Nobel Prize in Medicine 1970, born in Leipzig, 1929 study, 1934 M.D. 1990 Dr. h. c.

Theodor Kocher
Nobelpreis für Medizin 1909, Mitglied der Medizinischen Gesellschaft in Leipzig.
Nobel Prize in Medicine 1909, member of the Medical Society in Leipzig.

Lev Landau
Nobelpreis für Physik 1962, Anfang der 1930er-Jahre an Heisenbergs Institut in Leipzig.
Nobel Prize in Physics 1962, in early 1930s at Heisenberg's institute in Leipzig.

John Macleod
Nobelpreis für Medizin 1923, befasste sich in Leipzig zwei Jahre mit Physiologischer Chemie.
Nobel Prize in Medicine 1923, engaged in physiological chemistry in Leipzig for two years.

Theodor Mommsen
Literaturnobelpreis 1902, wirkte 1848/49 in Leipzig als Professor für Römisches Recht.
Nobel Prize in Literature 1902, Professor of Roman Law in Leipzig 1848/49.

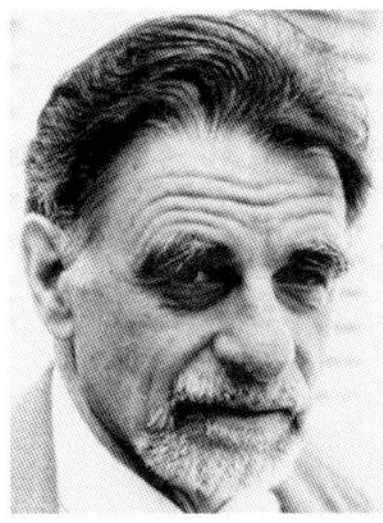

Alexander Müller
Nobelpreis für Physik 1987, Ehrendoktor 2000, enge Kontakte zum Bereich Festkörperphysik.
Nobel Prize in Physics 1987, Dr. h. c. 2000, close ties to solid state physics division.

Robert S. Mulliken
Nobelpreis für Chemie 1966, arbeitete am Leipziger Institut von Werner Heisenberg.
Nobel Prize in Chemistry 1966, worked at the institute of Werner Heisenberg in Leipzig.

Walther Nernst
Nobelpreis für Chemie 1920, Assistent bei Wilhelm Ostwald und Privatdozent.
Nobel Prize in Chemistry 1920, assistant to Wilhelm Ostwald and private lecturer.

Wilhelm Ostwald
Nobelpreis für Chemie 1909, Begründer und Professor der Physikalischen Chemie.
Nobel Prize in Chemistry 1909, Founder and Professor of Physical Chemistry.

Ivan P. Pavlov
Nobelpreis für Medizin 1904, arbeitete 1884 bis 1886 am Physiologischen Institut in Leipzig.
Nobel Prize in Medicine 1904, worked from 1884 to 1886 at the Physiological Institute in Leipzig.

Fritz Pregl
Nobelpreis für Chemie 1923, zuvor Mitarbeit am Leipziger Institut von Wilhelm Ostwald.
Nobel Prize in Chemistry 1923, previously involved with institute of Wilhelm Ostwald in Leipzig.

Isidor Isaac Rabi
Nobelpreis für Physik 1944, studierte Ende der 1920er-Jahre an Heisenbergs Institut.
Nobel Prize in Physics 1944, studied at Heisenberg's institute in late 1920s.

Theodore W. Richards
Nobelpreis für Chemie 1914, experimentierte bei Ostwald auf Gebiet der Elektrochemie.
Nobel Prize in Chemistry 1914, experimented in the field of electrochemistry under Ostwald.

Nathan Söderblom
Friedensnobelpreis 1930, von 1912 bis 1914 in Leipzig Professor für Religionsgeschichte.
Nobel Peace Prize 1930, from 1912 to 1914 Professor of History of Religion in Leipzig.

Gustav Stresemann
Friedensnobelpreis 1926, Studium und Promotion an der Philosophischen Fakultät in Leipzig.
Nobel Peace Prize 1926, study and doctorate at the Faculty of Philosophy Leipzig.

Sin-Itiro Tomonaga
Nobelpreis für Physik 1965, studierte bei Heisenberg Kernphysik und Quantenfeldtheorie.
Nobel Prize in Physics 1965, studied nuclear physics and quantum field theory under Heisenberg.

John H. van Vleck
Nobelpreis für Physik 1977, kam aus den USA ans Leipziger Institut von Werner Heisenberg.
Nobel Prize in Physics 1977, came from the U.S. to the institute of Werner Heisenberg in Leipzig.

Otto Wallach
Nobelpreis für Chemie 1910, erhielt 1907 die Ehrendoktorwürde der Leipziger Universität.
Nobel Prize in Chemistry 1910, received 1907 an honorary doctorate from the University of Leipzig.

DIE UNIVERSITÄT IM ÜBERBLICK
THE UNIVERSITY AT A GLANCE

KONTAKTADRESSEN CONTACT ADDRESSES

Rektorat
Rector's Office
Büro des Rektors
Ritterstraße 26
04109 Leipzig
Telefon +49 341 97-30000
rektorat@uni-leipzig.de

Pressestelle
Press Office
Ritterstraße 26
04109 Leipzig
Telefon +49 341 97-35020
presse@uni-leipzig.de

Eingang zum Rektoratsgebäude in der Ritterstraße.
Entrance to the Rector's Office building on Ritterstraße.

Akademisches Auslandsamt
International Office
Goethestraße 6
04109 Leipzig
Telefon +49 341 97-32020
aaa@uni-leipzig.de

Öffentlichkeitsarbeit
Public Relations
Ritterstraße 26
04109 Leipzig
Telefon +49 341 97-35000
oeffentlichkeitsarbeit@uni-leipzig.de

Forschungskontaktstelle
Research Promotion and Technology Transfer Assistance
Ritterstraße 26
04109 Leipzig
Telefon +49 341 97-35000
fkst@uni-leipzig.de

StudentInnenRat
Student Council
Universitätsstraße 1
04109 Leipzig
Telefon +49 341 97-37850
sp@stura.uni-leipzig.de

Zentrale Studienberatung
Student Guidance and Counselling Centre
Goethestraße 6
04109 Leipzig
Telefon +49 341 97-32005
zsb@uni-leipzig.de

Studentenwerk Leipzig
Student Services Leipzig
Goethestraße 6
04109 Leipzig
Telefon +49 341 96-59660
info@studentenwerk-leipzig.de

FAKULTÄTEN FACULTIES

Theologische Fakultät
Faculty of Theology
Otto-Schill-Straße 2
04109 Leipzig
Telefon +49 341 97-35400
dekanat@theologie.uni-leipzig.de

Juristenfakultät
Faculty of Law
Burgstraße 27
04109 Leipzig
Telefon +49 341 97-35100
simue@rz.uni-leipzig.de

Fakultät für Geschichte, Kunst- und Orientwissenschaften
Faculty of History, Art and Oriental Studies
Schillerstraße 6
04109 Leipzig
Telefon +49 341 97-35100
dekgko@rz.uni-leipzig.de

Philologische Fakultät
Faculty of Philology
Beethovenstraße 15
04107 Leipzig
Telefon +49 341 97-37300
dekphilo@rz.uni-leipzig.de

Erziehungswissenschaftliche Fakultät
Faculty of Education
Karl-Heine-Straße 22b
04229 Leipzig
Telefon +49 341 97-31400
dekanat.fakerz@uni-leipzig.de

Fakultät für Sozialwissenschaften und Philosophie
Faculty of Social Sciences and Philosophy
Beethovenstraße 15
04107 Leipzig
Telefon +49 341 97-35600
foerster@rz.uni-leipzig.de

Wirtschaftswissenschaftliche Fakultät
Faculty of Economics
Grimmaische Straße 12
04109 Leipzig
Telefon +49 341 97-33500
dekanat@wifa.uni-leipzig.de

Sportwissenschaftliche Fakultät
Faculty of Sports Science
Jahnallee 59
04109 Leipzig
Telefon +49 341 97-31600
spodekan@rz.uni-leipzig.de

Medizinische Fakultät
Faculty of Medicine
Liebigstraße 27b
04103 Leipzig
Telefon +49 341 97-15930
dekanat@medizin.uni-leipzig.de

Fakultät für Mathematik und Informatik
Faculty of Mathematics and Computer Science
Johannisgasse 26
04103 Leipzig
Telefon +49 341 97-32100
matinf@math.uni-leipzig.de

Fakultät für Biowissenschaften, Pharmazie und Psychologie
Faculty of Biosciences, Pharmacy and Psychology
Brüderstraße 32
04103 Leipzig
Telefon +49 341 97-36700
dekanat.bio@uni-leipzig.de

Fakultät für Physik und Geowissenschaften
Faculty of Physics and Earth Sciences
Linnéstraße 5
04103 Leipzig
Telefon +49 341 97-32400
dekan@physik.uni-leipzig.de

Fakultät für Chemie und Mineralogie
Faculty of Chemistry and Mineralogy
Johannisallee 29
04103 Leipzig
Telefon +49 341 97-36000
dekanat@chemie.uni-leipzig.de

Veterinärmedizinische Fakultät
Faculty of Veterinary Medicine
An den Tierkliniken 19
04103 Leipzig
Telefon +49 341 97-38000
dekanat@vetmed.uni-leipzig.de

AUSGEWÄHLTE EINRICHTUNGEN SELECTED FACILITIES

Biotechnologisch-Biomedizinisches Zentrum
Centre for Biotechnology and Biomedicine
Deutscher Platz 5
04103 Leipzig
Telefon: +49 341 97-31300
kontakt@bbz.uni-leipzig.de

Deutsches Literaturinstitut
Institute of German Literature
Wächterstraße 34
04107 Leipzig
Telefon +49 341 97-30300
dll@uni-leipzig.de

Forschungsakademie Leipzig
Research Academy Leipzig
Otto-Schill-Straße 2
04109 Leipzig
Telefon +49 341 97-32350
ral@uni-leipzig.de

Interdisziplinäres Zentrum für Bioinformatik
Interdisciplinary Centre for Bioinformatics
Härtelstraße 16–18
04107 Leipzig
Telefon +49 341 97-16670
kontakt@izbi.uni-leipzig.de

Sprachenzentrum
Foreign Language Centre
Klostergasse 3
04109 Leipzig
Telefon +49 341 97-30270
sprachenzentrum@uni-leipzig.de

Studienkolleg Sachsen
Preparatory College for International Students
Lumumbastraße 4
04105 Leipzig
Telefon +49 341 97-30242
burska@rz.uni-leipzig.de

Zentrum für Höhere Studien
Centre for Advanced Studies
Emil-Fuchs-Straße 1
04105 Leipzig
Telefon +49 341 97-30230
zhs@uni-leipzig.de

Universitätsrechenzentrum
University Computer Centre
Neumarkt 9–19
04109 Leipzig
Telefon +49 341 97-33300
urz@uni-leipzig.de

Translationszentrum für Regenerative Medizin
Translational Centre for Regenerative Medicine
Philipp-Rosenthal-Straße 55
04103 Leipzig
Telefon +49 341 97-39600
info@trm.uni-leipzig.de

Zentrum für Medien und Kommunikation
Centre for Media and Communications
Emil-Fuchs-Straße 1
04105 Leipzig
Telefon +49 341 97-35850
zmk@uni-leipzig.de

Zentrum für internationale Wirtschaftsbeziehungen
Centre for International Economic Relations
Universitätsstraße 16
04109 Leipzig
Telefon +49 341 97-30221
ziw@uni-leipzig.de

Zentrum für Magnetische Resonanz
Centre for Magnetic Resonance
Linnéstraße 5
04103 Leipzig
Telefon +49 341 97-32503
mrz@uni-leipzig.de

Zentrum für Lehrerbildung und Schulforschung
Centre for Teacher Education and School Research
Marschnerstraße 29/Haus 4
04109 Leipzig
Telefon +49 341 97-30481
zls@uni-leipzig.de

Zentrum für Frauen und Geschlechterforschung
Centre for Women's and Gender Studies
Beethovenstraße 15
04107 Leipzig
Telefon +49 341 97-37406
frages@rz.uni-leipzig.de

Zentrum für Hochschulsport
Centre for University Sports
Jahnallee 59/Haus I
04109 Leipzig
Telefon +49 341 97-30320
zfhsekr@uni-leipzig.de

Leipziger Universitätsmusik
Leipzig University Music
Goldschmidtstraße 12
04103 Leipzig
Telefon +49 341 97-30190
unimusik@uni-leipzig.de

Kustodie
Curator's Office
Hainstraße 11
04109 Leipzig
Telefon +49 341 97-30170
kustodie@uni-leipzig.de

Universitätsbibliothek
University Library
Beethovenstraße 6
04107 Leipzig
Telefon +49 341 97-30577
auskunft@ub.uni-leipzig.de

Universitätsarchiv
University Archives
Oststraße 40–42
04317 Leipzig
Telefon +49 341 9904920
archiv@uni-leipzig.de

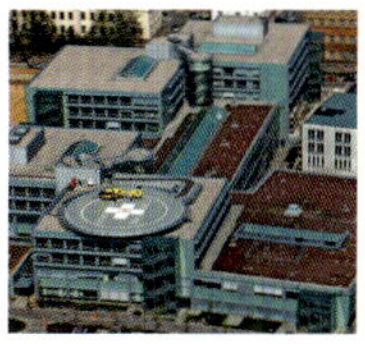

Universitätsklinikum Leipzig
University Hospital Leipzig
Philipp-Rosenthal-Straße 27
04103 Leipzig
Telefon +49 341 97-109
info@uniklinik-leipzig.de

MUSEEN UND AUSGEWÄHLTE SAMMLUNGEN
MUSEUMS AND SELECTED COLLECTIONS

Ägyptisches Museum
Egyptian Museum
Burgstraße 21
04109 Leipzig
Telefon +49 341 97-37010
fischere@uni-leipzig.de

Museum für Musikinstrumente
Museum for Musical Instruments
Johannisplatz 5–11
04103 Leipzig
Telefon +49 341 97-30750
musik.museum@uni-leipzig.de

Antikenmuseum
Antiques Museum
Alte Nikolaischule
Nikolaikirchhof 2
04109 Leipzig
Telefon +49 341 97-30700
klarch@rz.uni-leipzig.de

Geologisch-Paläontologische Sammlung
Geological-Paleontological Collection
Talstraße 35
04103 Leipzig
Telefon +49 341 97-32805
gmueller@rz.uni-leipzig.de

Botanischer Garten
Botanical Garden
Linnéstraße 1
04103 Leipzig
Telefon +49 341 97-38590
freiberg@uni-leipzig.de

Mineralogisch-Petrographische Sammlung
Mineralogical and Petrographic Collection
Scharnhorststraße 20
04275 Leipzig
Telefon +49 341 97-36256
hoebler@rz.uni-leipzig.de

Sammlung Ur- und Frühgeschichte
Collection of Prehistory and Early History
Ritterstraße 14
04109 Leipzig
Telefon +49 341 97-37051
rieckhoff@uni-leipzig.de

Lehrsammlung Anatomie
Anatomy Teaching Collection
Liebigstraße 13
04103 Leipzig
Telefon +49 341 97-22003
Christine.Feja@medizin.uni-leipzig.de

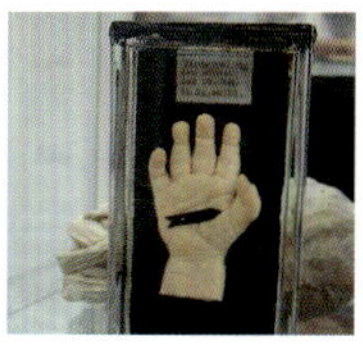

Lehrsammlung Pathologie
Pathology Teaching Collection
Liebigstraße 26
04103 Leipzig
Telefon +49 341 97-15000
info@uniklinik-leipzig.de

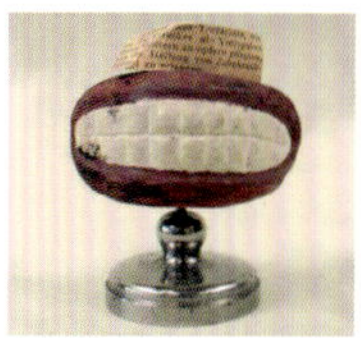

Medizinhistorische Sammlung
Collection of Medical History
Käthe-Kollwitz-Straße 82
04109 Leipzig
Telefon +49 341 97-25606
fahrs@medizin.uni-leipzig.de